THE EVERYTHING KIDS' SOCCER BOOK

Rules, techniques, and more about your favorite sport!

Deborah W. Crisfield

Adams Media Corporation
Avon, Massachusetts

EDITORIAL
Publishing Director: Gary M. Krebs
Managing Editor: Kate McBride
Copy Chief: Laura MacLaughlin
Acquisitions Editor: Cheryl Kimball
Development Editor: Michael Paydos

PRODUCTION
Production Director: Susan Beale
Production Manager: Michelle Roy Kelly
Series Designer: Colleen Cunningham
Layout and Graphics: Arlene Apone,
Paul Beatrice, Brooke Camfield,
Colleen Cunningham, Daria Perreault,
Frank Rivera

An Everything® Series Book.
Everything® is a registered trademark of Adams Media Corporation.

Published by Adams Media Corporation
57 Littlefield Street, Avon, MA 02322. U.S.A.
www.adamsmedia.com

ISBN: 1-58062-642-4

Printed in the United States of America.

J I H G F E D C B

Library of Congress Cataloging-in-Publication Data

Crisfield, Deborah.
　　The everything kids' soccer book / by Debbie Crisfield.
　　　　p.　　cm.
　　Contents: Soccer rules!—Control freak!—Getting your kicks—Dynamite
dribbling—In the net—On the attack—Defense—The soccer body—Games to
play—Going pro.
　　ISBN 1-58062-642-4
　　1. Soccer—Juvenile literature. [1. Soccer.] I. Title
GV943.25 .C75　　　　　　　　　　　　　　　　　　　2002
762.334—dc21　　　　　　　　　　　　　　　　　　　2001055308

Cover illustrations by Dana Regan.
Interior illustrations by Kurt Dolber.
Puzzles by Beth Blair.

Puzzle Power Software by Centron Software Technologies, Inc. was used to create puzzle grids.

This book is available at quantity discounts for bulk purchases.
For information, call 1-800-872-5627.

See the entire Everything® series at *everything.com*.

B&T 3/3/04   14.95

DEDICATION

For the Yellow Lightning Squirters

Contents

Acknowledgements

I'd like to thank Carrie Wickenden for her knowledge, Emma Wake for her coaching skills, Sophie Tournier and Werner Huygen for their research, Cheryl Kimball for her flexibility, Mrs. Fisher's 2001 kindergarten class for their insights, and as always, JAC, JDC, CBC, Otis, Piggy, and Heidi.

Introduction

Soccer can be found in more countries than any other sport in the world, and no other game is played by more people. It's the fastest growing sport in the United States, and it's the second most popular game for kids in this country (behind basketball). Yes, soccer is on top of the world, and you are on top of this exciting trend.

This book will help you become a super soccer player. If you've never played before, you'll get step-by-step instructions on every skill. And if you've already spent some time on the ball, the games and drills will help you improve your skills.

The first chapter covers some of the history of soccer and all of the rules, field markings, and equipment. If you're a little confused about the offside rule, look in Chapter 1.

The skills begin in Chapter 2. This is where you'll learn how to control the ball, the first step for any soccer player. Passing skills and strategy are discussed in Chapter 3, and dribbling is in Chapter 4. By the time you've read this far, you should be able to move the ball down the field like a pro.

There are a few among you who are daredevils, I'm sure. You folks don't mind being the center of attention, diving on the ground, and jumping hard into a group of attackers. You are goalkeepers. From cutting the angle to stopping the toughest of shots—all of the essential goal-tending info is in Chapter 5.

Once you've learned to move the ball, it's time to develop your soccer brain. You need to know how to think like a soccer player. Chapters 6 and 7 help you understand field positions, from forward to midfielder to defender. Staying fit and avoiding injuries are covered in Chapter 8.

We'll also have some fun. There's a whole chapter on all different types of soccer games you can play; it's Chapter 9. Finally, in Chapter 10 you'll learn what it takes to go pro.

Every chapter is filled with games and other fun things for you to do while you learn about the world's favorite sport. Kick back and enjoy!

Okay, so we know that soccer rules, but what are the soccer rules?

Soccer is about as simple as it gets. To play, you need a field, two goals, and a ball. That's it. The goals don't even have to be official goals. Cones, T-shirts, even a couple of trees will do the trick.

And talk about easy! Basically, it's no hands allowed. Kick the ball into the opponent's goal. Pretty simple, huh? Now just think about the rules for soccer compared to the rules for baseball or football. Even three-year-olds can learn the basic rules of soccer, but there are many grownups who still can't figure out baseball.

You'll probably want to know a few more rules than the average three-year-old. Like, what's the deal with the offside rule? And how do you do a kickoff? And what are those yellow and red cards I keep hearing about?

Read on for the answers, but don't worry. Soccer really is still as simple as you thought it was.

The Object of the Game

Go for the goal! That's the whole point of the game. Two teams, each with a goal to defend, battle to get the soccer ball into the opponent's goal. The winning team is the one with the most goals when the time runs out—two forty-five-minute halves. Of course, when you start playing, the halves won't be that long. The length of the game, the size of the ball, the size of the field, and even the number of players changes according to how old you are. (See the table on page 5.)

Soccer is played with one ball and two teams of eleven players each: ten field players and one goalkeeper. The goalkeeper wears a different colored shirt and is allowed to use his or her hands to touch the ball. The ten field players generally fall into one of three categories:

Defenders—Keep the ball from getting into the goal
Midfielders—Provide a link between defenders and forwards
Forwards—Shoot the ball into the opponent's goal

As you can see, each position has a job to do. You'll find more detailed descriptions in Chapters 6 and 7.

The Ball

Thousands of years ago, a soccer ball could be anything, as long as it was round and it rolled. Here are some things that people used for soccer balls:

- Animal skins filled with grass
- Coconuts
- Human skulls
- Pigs' bladders

Today, in many poorer countries, soccer players still have to make their own soccer balls. What would you use if you didn't have a soccer ball? List three things around your house that might make a good soccer ball.

Just for Fun

For a fun variation on soccer, try to play the way they did in olden times. Go to a park near your house and set up two goals, one on each side of the park. Try to get as many people involved as you can and see what fun it is to have to dribble and pass around trees, playground equipment, and backstops.

_____

_____

_____

FuN FACT

Less Is More

Many younger teams play with seven or nine on a side. Because younger players haven't learned to spread out, this makes the field less crowded. It also gives each player more opportunities to touch the ball.

Soccer balls come in many sizes and in several different designs. The traditional ball is called a Size 5 ball and consists of thirty-two leather panels: twelve are pentagonal (five-sided) and twenty are hexagonal (six-sided). It's about 27 inches in diameter and weighs about 15 ounces.

There are also several other popular designs now. Go on a hunt. See what other designs you can find. Copy them here:

Jokin' Around

Two boys were playing with a new soccer ball outside their house.

"Hey," shouted their mother, "where did you get that soccer ball?"

"We found it," replied one of the boys.

"Are you sure it was lost?" asked the mother.

"Yes," replied the boy, "we saw some people looking for it."

You'll use a Size 4 ball, a Size 5 ball, and maybe a Size 3 ball in your soccer-playing career. The following table shows how ball size, field size, goal size, and length of the game change according to how old you are. The age group you play in is determined by your age on August 1; so a U8 team means the players are under eight years old as of August 1. Most youth leagues begin play in September.

If you're interested in soccer, you'll definitely want to get your own ball. Nothing will help your soccer playing more than getting used to how the ball bounces around your foot.

AGE	BALL SIZE	FIELD SIZE	GOAL SIZE	LENGTH OF GAME
U6	3	20 x 30 yds.	4 x 6 ft.	20-minute halves
U8	3	30 x 50 yds.	6 x 12 ft.	20-minute halves
U10	4	50 x 70 yds.	6 x 18 to 7 x 21 ft.	25-minute halves
U11–U12	4	100 x 50 to 120 x 80 yds.	8 x 24 ft.	30-minute halves
U13–U14	5	same	same	35-minute halves
U15–U16	5	same	same	40-minute halves
U17–Adult	5	same	same	45-minute halves

Spelling Ball

How many words can you find in this soccer ball grid? You may start at any letter, then move from space to the next touching space in any direction, spelling out a word as you go. You may double back and use a letter more than once in a word (you can spell "eve"), but you may not use the same letter twice in a row (you can't spell "sleep").

The 10-letter BONUS word completes this phrase: Playing soccer is much more fun than watching _____!

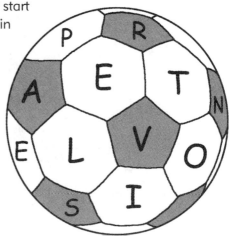

SCORE:
10 words = Starter
20 words = Pro
30 words = World Cup

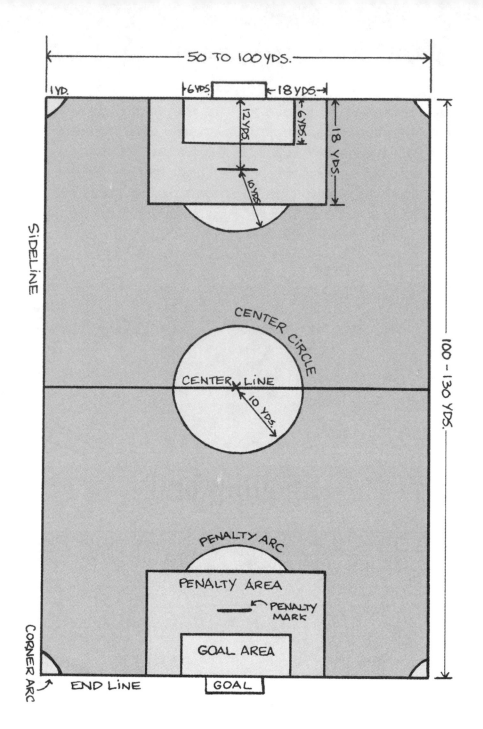

Dimensions of a soccer field

Let's Play

In each of the soccer balls is the scrambled name of something you need to play soccer—minus one letter! Add the missing letter to complete the word. Then arrange the missing letters to spell one more important piece of soccer equipment.

1.
2.
3.
4.
5.
6.

1. _____

2. _____

3. _____

4. _____

5. _____

6. _____

BONUS: _____

The Field

The size of a soccer field is flexible. Remember, back in the Middle Ages, the goals could be as far as 10 miles apart. The rules are a little more rigid now, but fields can still be different sizes.

Officially, the field should be between 100 and 130 yards long, and between 50 and 100 yards wide. But you could never have a square field; that is, 100 by 100. The length always has to be longer than the width. The goal is 8 yards wide and 8 feet high. Take a look at the following picture to see all the measurements.

Even though these are the official measurements, your games might be played on a much smaller field. If you're playing on a team that has fewer than eleven on a side, then the field will be smaller.

The Big Field

The official size for an international match is a field that is 100 to 110 meters long (which is 110 to 120 yards) and 64 to 75 meters wide (which is 70 to 80 yards).

The Kickoff

Kickoffs are used for three different events.

1. At the start of a game
2. At the start of the second half
3. After a goal has been scored

The ball is placed in the center of the center circle. Each team must start the game on their side of the field. The defending team must also stay out of the center circle. The other team has at least one and often two players up near the ball. At the referee's whistle, the game begins. The ball is moved and then it's up for grabs. The player who kicked the ball first may not touch it again until someone else has touched it.

Playing the Game

Once the ball is in play, the teams try to move the ball up the field toward the opponent's goal. A player may move the ball with any part of his body except for the parts between the shoulders and the fingertips. A player can keep the ball or pass it off to another player. The team without the ball does its best to steal the ball and stop the opponents from shooting.

Play is only stopped when the ball goes into the goal or rolls out-of-bounds (the entire ball must be beyond the outer edge of the line) or when a foul is committed. Play can also be stopped by the referee for any reason he or she determines. The clock is never stopped, unless there is a serious injury.

Foul Play

There are a whole bunch of actions that will cause a referee to blow her whistle. See how many you can name. If you get one or two, you're a soccer starter; three or four, you're a soccer smarty; five or more, you're a soccer star. Don't peek at the list until you've tried it yourself.

- Charging
- Handling the ball
- Hitting
- Holding
- Kicking
- Pushing
- Tripping

Dangerous play (like a high kick near someone's head)
Goalkeeper offenses
Interfering with the goalkeeper
Obstruction
Violating the offside rule
Ungentlemanly conduct (bad behavior)

Those are the main ones. If a player commits one of these fouls, the other team gets a free kick. There are a few other minor fouls, but they probably won't be an issue for you unless you go pro.

Notice that the fouls are divided into two groups. For the first group of fouls, the team gets a direct kick. A direct kick means that the team can kick it right at the goal without anyone but the kicker touching the ball. If the player commits one of these fouls in the penalty box, look out! It's time for a penalty kick. Not only can the player kick it directly at the goal, but he gets to do it from a mere 12 yards away, and the other team is allowed no defense but the goalie.

WORDS to KNOW

obstruction: This call means that you've placed your body between your opponent and the ball without going after the ball yourself. You might be trying to keep your opponent from saving the ball if it's going out-of-bounds or to give your goalie a chance to pick it up. Either way, it's not allowed. You can throw your body in front of another player, as long as you are actually going after the ball.

FUN FACT

It's the Ref's Call

There are times when a referee might not call an obvious foul. This usually happens when the team that is fouled has the advantage after the foul is committed. For instance, if they were about to score, it would be unfair to stop play and set up a free kick just because the other team fouled. In fact, it might encourage some players to behave badly and try to foul whenever the other team gets close to the goal.

The fouls in the second group are not quite as serious, so the team gets an indirect kick. That means that at least two players need to touch the ball before it goes into the goal.

Pick a Card

If a player displays really bad behavior, is not playing fairly, or continues to commit the same foul again and again, the referee might pull out his cards. He has two cards: one yellow and one red. Think of them like a stoplight. The yellow one is a warning that the red one isn't far behind. The yellow one usually comes out first, but next time it happens, the red card gets pulled. The red card means that the player is kicked off the field and she can't come back in. In fact, the player may not be able to play in the next game as well. Just imagine what the sport of hockey would be like if it had the same rules as soccer.

Here are some other things that will get you an automatic red card:

- Violence
- Spitting
- Blocking a goal with your hands if you're not the keeper (which also gives the team an automatic goal)
- Bad language
- Receiving a second yellow card in the same game
- Foul play
- Denying an obvious goal-scoring chance by committing an offense punishable by a direct or free kick

FUN FACT

Red Cards Aplenty

In a match in Paraguay on June 1, 1993, a referee gave twenty players a red card and sent them off the field. They had to stop the game due to lack of players.

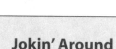

Jokin' Around

An angry midfielder snarled at the referee. "What would I happen if I called you a blind idiot who couldn't make the right call to save his life?"

"That would be a red card for you."

"And if I didn't say it but only thought it?"

"That's different. If you only thought it but didn't say anything, I couldn't do a thing."

"Well, we'll leave it like that, then, shall we?" smiled the player.

Out-of-Bounds

Sometimes play is stopped for a less dramatic reason than a foul: the ball has simply rolled out-of-bounds, which means the entire ball has rolled all the way over the line. There are three different ways to get it back in play, depending on how it went out. See if you can match the restart from Column A with the list in Column B.

COLUMN A

A. Throw-in

B. Goal kick

C. Corner kick

COLUMN B

1. The defending team kicks the ball over the goal (or end) line.

2. The ball goes over the touchline (or sideline).

3. The attacking team kicks the ball over the goal line.

If you guessed A–2, B–3, and C–1, you're right!

Make sure you pay attention to the referee's whistle. You don't want to pick up a ball that you think is over the line when it's really not. Otherwise, the other team gets a free kick because of your "handball." And keep in mind, a ball is not out-of-bounds until it has rolled completely over the line. If it's still touching part of the line, then it's still in play.

Throw-ins

Let's talk about the throw-in first. When a player kicks the ball over a **touchline,** the other team gets to throw the ball back in. But don't just wind up and give it a toss. There are a lot of rules you must follow.

Tip

Sometimes you'll hear people call the touchline the sideline or say offsides Instead of offside. But those are American football terms, and you're playing soccer.

WORDS to KNOW

touchline: Also known as the sideline. One of the two longer lines that are the boundaries of the field of play. The lines are included as part of the field of play.

goal line: Also known as the endline. One of the two shorter lines that form the boundaries of the field of play. The lines are included as part of the field.

1. Both feet must be on the ground when you let go of the ball.
2. You must throw the ball equally with both hands.
3. Both hands must start from behind your head and come all the way over.
4. Your body must face the way you're throwing.

Most new players have a hard time learning how to do the throw-in properly. You can read the rules and look at the following picture, but the best thing to do is to get outside with a friend and practice it. Make sure you have someone watch you, though, because you don't want to be practicing an incorrect throw!

The throw-in

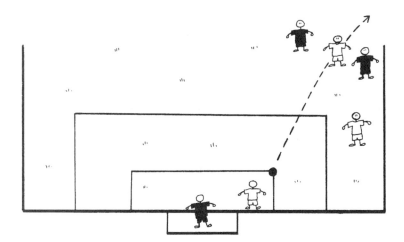

The goal kick

Goal Kicks

When the attacking team kicks the ball over the **goal line,** the defending team gets a free kick. This is called a goal kick. Sometimes new players call this a "goalie" kick. That's not right. In fact, at the lower levels of soccer, the goalie is the last player who should be taking this kick! The kick might not go very far and you want the goalie in the goal protecting it from whatever is coming back at you.

For a goal kick, the ball should be placed anywhere within the 6-yard box. Most players put it on the corner of the box, because they'll probably want to kick it out to the side. That spot gives them the most advantage as you can see.

Corner Kicks

If the defenders kick the ball over the goal line, something very different happens. It's a corner kick. The attacking team places the ball in the corner of the field, where the touchline and the goal line meet.

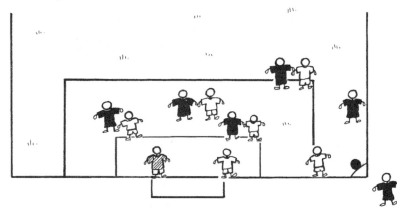

The corner kick

The ball can go directly into the goal on a corner kick, though it takes a rather talented kicker to manage that.

> **Tip**
>
> If you're defending the goal and can choose whether to kick the ball out over the touchline or the goal line, always choose the touchline. A corner kick is a much bigger advantage to the other team than a throw-in.

> "I just don't understand," a new soccer player complained. "One game I play great, then the next game I'm terrible."
>
> "Well," said his mom, "why don't you just play every other game?"

What on Earth Is Offside?

And now we've reached the point in the rules where we get to learn about the offside rule. Offside is a complicated rule but a good one. Without the offside rule, teams would be able to have a player stand down near the other team's goal and just wait for the ball to come. Scoring a goal wouldn't be nearly as challenging.

So here's the nitty-gritty on the offside rule. First of all, you have to be on your opponent's half of the field. Then you must have either the ball or two players from the other team (the goalie counts as one) between you and the goal.

If not, you are offside.

There are three exceptions:

1. If you're not involved in the play (in other words, you're off picking dandelions). It's only if you go for the ball or are passed the ball that being in the offside position matters; otherwise, the referee probably won't call it. Nonetheless, it's a good idea to try to be aware of where the defenders are because you're not doing your team much good if you can't be involved in the play. And one of your teammates might even pass you the ball not noticing that you're offside. Then you've given the other team a free kick.
2. If it's a throw-in, goal kick, or corner kick. You can't be offside on one of these.
3. If the other team kicks the ball to you. Obviously this would be accidental and lucky you, you wouldn't be called offside. But don't plan for it.

The penalty for offside is an indirect free kick for the other team. Look at these pictures to help you understand this rule.

Pelé

The world's most famous soccer player is a Brazilian named Edson Arantes do Nascimento, better known as Pelé. He led the Brazil team to three World Cup victories in 1958, 1962, and again in 1970. Pelé was the only person ever to be on three World Cup teams. He was skilled at all parts of the game, but scoring was his specialty. In 1958, he scored 139 goals in one season! And he holds the world record for scoring 1,282 goals in his career. After he retired, Pelé was hired by the New York Cosmos to try to bring the excitement of soccer to the United States. It worked to some extent. People loved Pelé, but the league folded.

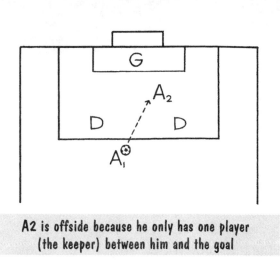

A2 is offside because he only has one player (the keeper) between him and the goal

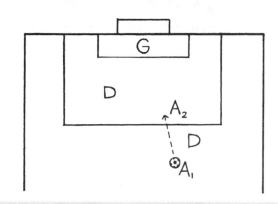

A2 is not offside because two players are closer to the goal

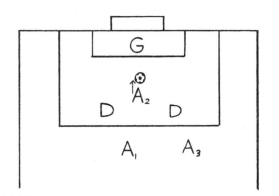

A2 is not offside because he is in control of the ball

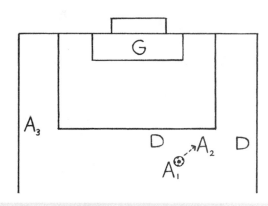

A3 is not offside because she's not involved in the play

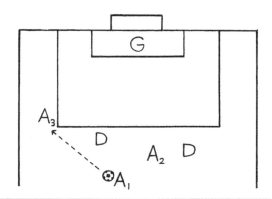

If A1 passes the ball, A3 is offside because there is only one player between him and the goal

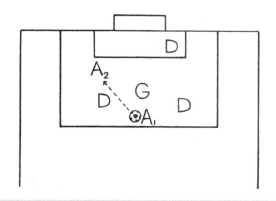

A2 is offside because there is only one player between her and the goal

What kind of tea
do bad soccer
players drink?

Penaltea!

For all the restarts—direct kicks, indirect kicks, throw-ins, corner kicks, and goal kicks—the referee will only blow the whistle once, when the ball goes out-of-bounds or when a foul has been committed. Don't wait for another whistle telling you when to kick or throw. That's up to you. In fact, usually the faster you do it the better. Don't give the defense a chance to set up. The only time a referee will make you wait for a second whistle is when a team is subbing.

And that's basically the rules and regulations in a nutshell. Now you just need to find out where soccer got its crazy name and then you're ready to learn some moves.

What's in a Name?

You might have heard that soccer is referred to as "football" in other countries. In which case, you're probably wondering why people in the United States call it "soccer." Where in the world did we get that name?

In England, during the early 1800s, there were two kinds of football games. One of them was called rugby football and the other was called association football because it was played by the rules set by **FIFA,** the Fédération Internationale de Football Association. Because association football was such a long name, people started calling it "assoc football" for short. That quickly turned into "soccer."

At the same time, American football was becoming popular. So people in the United States found it pretty handy to say "soccer" instead of association football. It kept things a little clearer. In England, however, the opposite happened. Rugby

WORDS to KNOW

FIFA: The *Fédération Internationale de Football* Association is the official soccer organization for world play. If a rule change is made, it's made by FIFA.

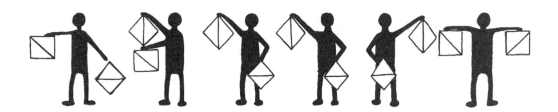

The word "soccer" in semaphores

football was shortened to just rugby, and so association football became just plain old "football." The assoc or soccer name was just dropped. The rest of the world didn't have the two-sport confusion, and they just called the sport football. It looks a little different in each language, but it's still the same game.

Here are the words for "soccer" in other languages:

Online Kick

If you want a more detailed description of the rules of soccer, including all of the latest changes, go to FIFA's Web site at *www.fifa.com.*

Futbol in Spanish
Voetbal in Dutch (Holland)
Fussball in German
Fotboll in Swedish
Calcio or *futbol* in Italian
Aqsaqtuk in Eskimo

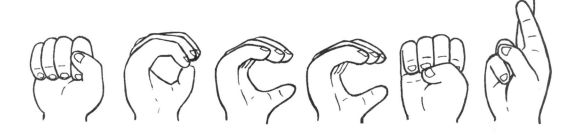

The word "soccer" in sign language

Soccer is all about control. The team that controls the ball controls the game. Think about it. If you never let the other team have the ball, how can they score? Of course, that's completely unrealistic I know, but you can still try, right?

Knowing that you need to control the ball and actually getting it under control are two different things entirely. How do you get that big bouncing ball to behave? Take a look at some of the tips in this chapter and then get out and practice, practice, practice!

Do you think soccer is a game played with your feet? Think again! You can use all sorts of body parts to control the ball. Circle the parts of the body that you think soccer players can use to control the ball:

Chest	Head
Elbows	Knees
Feet	Shoulders
Fist	Stomach
Hands	Thighs

If you circled chest, feet, head, stomach, and thighs, you're right! You definitely don't want to use anything that's part of your arms! It's off-limits from shoulders to fingertips. The knees were the tricky item in the list. It's not against the rules to use your knees, but it is certainly not a good idea if you're trying to control the ball.

But if the ball is rolling, bouncing, or flying through the air, how on earth do you get it under your control? The technique is called **trapping,** no matter which part of the body you choose to use.

Just for Fun

If you have three people, try a good old-fashioned game of Monkey in the Middle. Two of you team up and try to keep possession of the ball while passing it back and forth. The third person does her best to get it away from you.

trapping: Stopping the soccer ball and getting it under control with any part of the body.

Feet First

Let's start with the feet, since the feet are used more than anything else to control the ball. And while we're starting simply, let's just have the ball sitting quietly in front of us, too. We don't need it to go bouncing around quite yet. You can move the ball forward, sideways, and backward just by giving it a short hard tap. When you do this while you're running, it's called **dribbling**, and it will be covered in great detail in Chapter 4.

But it's not often that the ball is just sitting there quietly waiting for you to move it. Usually it's in motion. Let's say it's rolling along the ground toward you. Your goal is to stop the ball so you can direct it the way you want it to go. So how do you do that? First, lift your foot up a few inches off the ground, about halfway up the soccer ball.

The foot is halfway up the soccer ball for a trap

Then at the instant the ball meets your foot, drop your foot back a little. By doing this, you're providing something to block the ball to get it to stop rolling, but it's not something hard that will cause the ball to bounce off in another direction.

Try looking at it this way. Picture a hard rolling ball hitting a wall. That ball is going to bounce right back in the opposite direction, right? You don't want your foot to be a wall. Instead you want your foot to be a big squishy pillow that the ball will sink into. Unfortunately, your foot isn't really a big squishy pillow, so you have to allow the ball to "sink into" your foot by moving your foot away from the ball.

FUN FACT

Ball Trap!

Many players trap the ball between the ground and the bottom of their cleats. In other words, they basically step on the ball. The upside of this trap is that the ball stops dead when you do it right. The downside is that it's really hard to do it right. Players end up stepping too hard, twisting their ankle, or missing the ball entirely. Until you're really good at soccer, leave this trap for the pros.

Trapping the ball out of the air

You and a friend should pass the ball back and forth to each other until you perfect this motion. Because after this, it just gets trickier. Like, for instance, when the ball is in the air. Let's say it's a big lofted ball heading down to the ground right in front of you. How are you going to get control of it? The concept is the same. Hold your foot out and up in the air so that the ball will land on it. Then, just as the ball hits your foot, drop your foot down or pull it away.

When you're taking the ball out of the air, be careful not to lose your balance. You'll be standing on one leg as you raise the other, so make sure that leg is steady and strong. Bend the knee slightly and don't forget even though you can't use your arms to touch the ball, you can certainly hold them out to help steady your body.

Again, the more you practice this, the better. You and a friend should now pick the ball up and toss it back and forth. Change the height of the tosses. Some should be big lobs coming way out of the sky, but others should be more like line drives coming in at knee level or a little higher.

If you are by yourself, you can still practice. Toss the ball into the air and "catch" it with your foot before it hits the ground.

Tip

Think of the ball as an egg or a water balloon that you don't want to break. That might help you treat it more gently.

Thighs

Most of the time when a ball is coming in at thigh level, you'll want to try to raise your foot high and trap it with your foot. But sometimes that's just too awkward or the ball is too high. You don't want to completely lose your balance, so you use your thigh to trap the ball. And you don't want to get called for dangerous play, if you kick too high toward another player's head.

When you're trapping with your thigh, make sure you're facing the ball. Then it's really the same concept as the foot, just a few feet higher. Raise your leg in the air and then as soon as the ball hits your thigh, drop it away.

Tip

By putting your arms out, you not only give yourself balance, but you also keep your arms and your hands out of the way of the ball so you aren't called for a handball.

Juggling

Now that you've learned to control the ball with your feet and your thighs, you can start **juggling.** Juggling is one the best ways you can practice good ball control. Now this doesn't mean I'm expecting you to keep six flaming torches in the air at once. Soccer juggling is a little different. It's only one ball. But you still need to keep it in the air.

Start by dropping the ball onto your foot or thigh. Then use both feet and both thighs to keep the ball in the air. Not only will you become quickly familiar with how the ball bounces, but it will also give you a great sense of how increased force makes the ball bounce away, while less force makes it drop in front of you. Understanding this concept is the key to trapping and ball control.

Here are a few juggling games to play:

1. *For one person:* Start by dropping the ball on your foot or thigh. Count how many times you can put the ball back up in the air without it touching the ground. Try to beat your own record.
2. *For two or more people:* If you each have a ball, see who can keep it up in the air longest. If you have only one ball, work together to try to beat your own juggling records.
3. *For three or more people with only one ball:* The group should stand in a fairly small circle. One person begins

WORDS to KNOW

juggling: Keeping the ball from touching the ground using your feet and thighs and even your head to pop the ball back up into the air.

Skill Master

This is two puzzles in one! First, get the soccer ball through the maze from START to GOAL. While you're doing that, carefully study the field full of practice players. Try to remember everything you see. Then turn to page 27 and answer the questions without looking back at the picture!

START

GOAL!

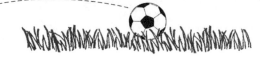

with the ball. He tosses to someone else in the circle. That person juggles the ball as long as he wants (it might be only once) and then sends it to another person in the circle using his foot or thigh or possibly head to do so. This continues until the ball hits the ground. The person who was juggling at the time is eliminated. If the ball was being passed from one person to another, then the group decides whether the ball hitting the ground is the fault of the receiver or the sender. The winner is the last one left.

4. *For three or more people with lots of balls:* All players except one have a ball. They begin juggling them. The one without the ball is the "hunter." He moves among the players waiting for a ball to drop. If one does, he goes after it, trying to gain control. And that's with feet only, by the way! If he gains control, then he gets to juggle and the person who lost it becomes the hunter. If you want to have a winner in this game, then you can have the original hunter remain as a hunter with the new hunter. The last one left is the winner.

When you become very good at juggling, then you can try starting the juggling without using your hands. Step on the ball, roll it back, get your foot under it, and pop it up. Then start juggling.

Jokin' Around

First Soccer Player: Boy, these new cleats sure hurt.

Second Soccer Player: That's because you're wearing them on the wrong feet.

First Soccer Player: I can't be. These are the only feet I have!

Speed Drill

How should a pass receiver be? This tiny picture puzzle shows how!

Julie Foudy

Julie Foudy is a captain on the U.S. National Team. As a midfielder and a playmaker, she led her team to World Cup victory in 1999, scoring one goal and three assists in the tournament. She also was a major factor in the U.S. team's silver medal win in the 2000 Olympics. Now she's making things happen for the San Diego Spirit.

Chest

Now let's go up a little higher. There are two ways to control the ball with your chest and your thigh. One is to apply the same principles that you learned for the feet and the thighs. "Catch" the ball with your body by immediately giving a little to cushion the ball when it hits. If you're doing it this way, you'll want to lean back, with your arms out at your sides to give you balance. After you "catch" the ball, then lean forward and drop the ball at your feet. This method is good if you need to have the ball tightly controlled in a small area.

The second way to trap a ball coming at chest level is to run through it; in other words, run right into it and keep running. Use your body like a big wall this time, and don't cushion the impact. The ball will bounce off your body, but if you hit it square on, then it should bounce off directly in front of you. Your body is generally soft enough that it won't bounce too far. So, if you are "running through it," you will quickly catch up to it. This is good if there's a little bit of space in front of you. Otherwise another player can snatch that ball up as soon as it bounces off you.

Trapping the ball with the chest

Running through the ball

First Touch

When you run through a ball, in some sense you are directing the ball with your body right from the start. In other words, at the first touch. Instead of dropping the ball at your feet, you're sending it forward. When you get to be a more experienced soccer player, you should practice this first-touch philosophy with every ball you get, whether it's with your feet, thigh, body, or head.

Directing the ball on your first touch can sometimes make all the difference when you're trying to get away from a defender. Notice where the defenders are, and think about where you'd like to put the ball. Sometimes it might be right in front of your feet, but other times, you might want to send it in a certain direction. In that case, you don't want your foot to be quite as cushiony. You'll want the ball to rebound off your foot instead. Position your foot so the rebound will be in the direction you want. Then as soon as the ball hits your foot, take off in that direction. You'll have the element of surprise in your favor and it might put you a step ahead.

That said, don't worry about directing the ball on the first touch until you've completely mastered the art of trapping. You need to develop a soft touch before you increase the resistance and make a harder touch that pushes the ball in a certain direction.

Skill Master Questions

1. How many players are on the field?
2. How many soccer balls are on the field?
3. What pattern does the goalie have on her shirt?
4. There is a player with her hair in a long braid. Where is she on the field?

BONUS: There are two players wearing the same uniform. What are their numbers?

Mom in sports shop: "May I have a soccer ball for my son?"

Salesperson: "Sorry madam, we don't do trades!"

Taking It in the Head

And now finally we get to the head. Some recent studies have suggested that heading the soccer ball can cause brain damage in very young kids. Their bodies are still growing and aren't able to cope with the repeated blows to the head that come with heading the ball. It is theorized that the damage comes from many repeated minor injuries (each time the ball bumps the head) that have a cumulative effect. The best advice is to keep practice to a minimum, stop immediately if you feel any pain, and pay attention to any lingering effects you might feel!

Heading is a big part of soccer. Anyone who loves soccer and is thinking of playing it as an adult is going to have to know about heading the ball. Because the ball is in the air a lot, heading is a huge part of the game, and you'll be at a big disadvantage if you have to wait for the ball to come down. Here is a quick overview.

Heading the Ball

There are three basic rules you should follow for heading the ball. Concentrate on these three things no matter what type of ball you're trying to head, and you'll be successful:

1. Hit the ball square in the middle of your forehead. Face balls hurt and scalp balls don't go anywhere but straight up.
2. Meet the ball. It will hurt less than if you wait and let it hit you.
3. Keep your eyes open and watch the ball all the way to your head.

Jokin' Around

A not-so-smart fan arrives at a soccer game partway through the second half.

"What's the score?" he asks his friend as he settles into his seat.

"Zero to zero," comes the reply.

"And what was the score at halftime?" he asks.

What You Can Do with a Well-Headed Ball

And here are a few things you can do with that perfect header:

1. *Trapping header:* Run through the ball. You're trying to get the ball out of the air and under your control. Hit the ball square in the middle of your forehead, as you point your face down to the ground.
2. *Defensive header:* In this case you want to get the ball as far away from your goal as possible. Arch your back, get your arms out for balance, and then snap forward at the last minute, meeting the ball square in the middle of your forehead.
3. *Shooting or passing header:* This is similar to a defensive header in force, but you may also want to direct it to one side or the other by hitting it not-so-square on the forehead.
4. *Diving header:* Only do this in front of the goal. And if you're not good with pain, don't try it at all. If there's a low ball in front of the goal that you think you can dive at and get your head on, go for it. Throw your arms out in front of you and dive toward the ball, meeting it with your forehead. After you hit the ground, get up immediately so your head isn't kicked by all the feet around the goal area.

Diving header

> What's the best place to shop for a soccer shirt?
>
> New Jersey!

Online Kick

If you're the kind of soccer fan who not only loves to play the game but also loves to collect sports cards of all your favorite professional soccer players, then there's a great Web site for you. It's *www.soccercards.com* and it has any soccer card you could ever imagine wanting.

Brian McBride

If you want to see a player who has learned the importance of using more than just his feet to control the ball, watch Columbus Crew star Brian McBride. Nobody plays the ball out of the air better than he does. He's up on the forward line just waiting for the ball to be crossed so he can head it into the goal. But don't make the mistake of thinking he can't use his feet. He's the all-time Columbus Crew top scorer, the top scorer for the Major League Soccer All-Star Game, and in the 1998 World Cup game against Iran, he scored the only U.S. goal.

I Spy Soccer

Be on the lookout for the word SOCCER hiding in this grid! There is only one time where all six letters appear in a row. Look forward, backward, up, down, and diagonally. It could be anywhere!

```
S R O S O S O C C E
O O R O S O C C E S
C E C C O C C O R O
C S O C E C E S O C
R O S E R E R O S S
S S O C C O S E O O
O C C S O C E C C C
C E R O C O C C C E
C O O C S E O O S E
E C O S R O C C O S
```

The final thing you need to know about heading the ball is that timing is everything. And like everything else, that's only going to come with practice. But unless you're a good foot taller than everyone else, most of your headers are going to come off of jumps. You need to time your jump just perfectly to beat your opponent to the ball.

That's easy, right? Perfect timing and perfect control on every touch. If you can do that, look out soccer world! There's a superstar coming up.

Mia Hamm

Without question, Mia Hamm is the most famous woman soccer player in the world. There are some who would argue that she is the world's best player, especially since she holds the international scoring record for both men and women! She also has so many assists that she would be considered one of the top ten scorers in U.S. history even if she never made a goal herself. She was part of the U.S. National Team that won the Women's World Cup in 1999, and now she plays for the Washington Freedom.

Tip

Practice makes perfect, so be sure to practice the different types of passing as much as you can. If you can't find a friend to do it with you, a wall or a backstop makes a great partner.

An announcer shouting GOOOOAAAALLLL!!!!!!!! A player ripping his shirt off in celebration. The drama of a shootout. Getting that elusive goal in soccer provides a thrill like no other. In basketball, you can score over 100 points in a game. Football games tend to be something like 26–18. Even baseball games, which usually have low scores, often end up with something like 6–5 by the end. But soccer is different. A 1–0 win is not uncommon, so the rare goal is extraordinarily sweet.

This chapter is going to show you all the skills you'll need to experience that sweet feeling yourself. You'll also learn how to pass the ball around the field, since most of the same skills are used whether you're shooting the ball or passing the ball. In the last chapter, you learned how to control the ball when it comes to you. In this one, you will learn how to get rid of it.

Perfect Passing

Soccer is a team sport, so it makes sense that sharing the ball among all your teammates is probably the best way to play. This sharing is called passing, and it's also the best way to move the ball toward the goal. Think of the other options.

- You could boot the ball halfway down the field. That would get the ball there faster, but who knows which team would end up with it.
- You could bring the ball down the field all by yourself. That would ensure that the ball stays in your possession, but it would take forever. And unless you're really skilled, there's a good chance that someone would steal it away from you.

So your best bet is to use a series of passes.

There are several different kinds of passes, but they all have a few things in common.

1. The first step in the pass, called a **plant,** is made with your non-kicking foot. This allows you to shift your weight as you are making your pass, which will give the pass more power.
2. Your planting foot must always be pointed in the direction you want the ball to go.
3. The pass must be crisp. A lazy slow dribbler is going to be intercepted in a second.
4. The pass must be accurate. If you don't get the ball to your teammate, the opponents will step in and steal it.
5. The pass should lead your teammate. Don't pass it to where she is now. Think of where she'll be in the next two seconds. Pass it a few feet in front of her, so she can keep running at the same pace.

Keep all these ideas in mind as you learn about the different types of passes.

The Push Pass

Many times your passes will be short, about 10 yards or less. For this pass, your best bet is to use the inside of your foot. This is called a **push pass.** Take a step toward the ball with your non-kicking foot, and plant that foot next to the ball. Your weight should be on this foot, which lets your other leg swing freely. As your body moves forward with this plant, turn your kicking foot sideways and lock it in an L-shaped position with your leg. If you think about turning your foot and leg into a hockey stick, it might help you to better picture what the push pass looks like. All the swing comes from your hips, not from your knee joint.

WORDS to KNOW

plant: A step toward the ball that shifts your weight forward and gives you more power for your kick.

Speed Drill

This tiny picture puzzle shows the important first step of any pass. What is it?

WORDS to KNOW

follow through: A term used in many sports. It means that the swinging motion doesn't stop with impact. The leg (or baseball bat or tennis racket) continues to move forward in the same direction.

push pass: A short accurate pass using the inside of the foot.

FUN FACT

Outside-of-the-Foot Pass

You can also use the outside of your foot to make a pass, but it will likely be no more than a nudge. You won't get much power using this part of the foot, but if your teammate is near enough it might allow you to escape a defender.

Now hit the ball squarely in the middle. If you hit it on the top of the ball, you'll lose much of your power. If you hit it low on the ball, it will pop up a little and have some backspin, which will cost you some distance.

You should already have your planting foot pointing in the direction you want the ball to go, and now you should **follow through** with your kicking foot in that same direction. Make sure you kick the ball hard enough to make it move quickly—no lazy little rollers that can be snagged by the defense.

The foot is halfway up the soccer ball for a trap

The **push pass** is the most accurate pass. The reason is that you use such a large part of your shoe to move the ball. It's hard not to hit it exactly where you want it because so much of your foot is involved. As long as you follow through to your target, the ball will go where you want it to go.

The Heel Pass

Frequently the best pass you have will be behind you. Your teammates are more likely to be open, and they may have more room to move the ball around and find the open man if there is pressure on you. Most of the time you'll have a few seconds to turn around and make a standard push pass; but sometimes, the pressure will be too intense, and you'll have to come up with another option. This is where the heel pass comes in.

To do a heel pass, simply give the ball a sharp hit with your heel. Make sure you keep your head down and watch your heel hit the ball squarely in the center. This is an easy pass to miss if you're not watching closely. If you don't hit the ball in the dead center, it's going to spin off to the side.

Don't make this pass unless you know someone is behind you. You won't be able to see the player, but he should be talking to you to let you know where he is. And never use it in front of the goal. It's too risky since you can't see who might be sneaking in to intercept the pass.

What do you call a soccer player who's half man and half horse?

A centaur forward!

Fast Pass

Use your instep to start the ball driving down the field to a teammate. Continue alternating foot to ball until the path reaches the goal at the other end of the field. You can move up and down, or side-to-side, but not diagonally. If you hit a player's hand, a foul is called and you have to start again!

Extra skill play: Using just your finger to trace the path, see how long it takes you to do this puzzle. Try again in 10 minutes and see if it takes you just as long. Try again ten minutes after that. What's your best time?

START

GOAL!

WORDS to KNOW

instep: The arched middle portion of the foot located directly in front of the ankle and under the shoelaces.

instep pass: Also called a shoelace pass, it's a powerful pass that lets the player loft the ball into the air by striking it with her instep.

FUN FACT

The Soccer-Style Kick

Many beginning players use their toes to kick the ball because it gives them more distance than the instep. This is a mistake. If you practice the instep pass, it won't take you long until it's just as powerful as the toe-poke, and it's certainly a whole lot more accurate, as a Hungarian football player named Pete Gogolak showed the NFL. Until he came along, the field goal kickers were kicking with their toes. Coming from Hungary, Pete had played soccer, not American football, so his long kicks were all soccer style. He was so successful that people started copying him. Now, a soccer style–instep kick is all you see.

The Long Ball

Many times in a soccer game, you'll see a teammate down the field who is wide open. A push pass isn't going to cut it. Now you're going to need the **instep pass**. It's also called the shoelace pass, because that's exactly the part of the foot you're going to use to kick it.

The instep pass is key for any soccer player. This is a much more powerful pass than the push pass, and it also lets you loft the ball into the air if you need to. Both of these come in pretty handy if you're trying to get the ball downfield quickly.

The instep pass

To kick the ball with your **instep,** you'll want to plant your foot in the same place as the push pass, about 2 or 3 inches out from the ball. In the instep pass, however, you're probably going to plant with more of a hop than a step.

Now, instead of holding your leg rigid, like a hockey stick, get your knee into the action. As you hop forward, your kicking leg swings backward, bending at the knee. Then, as soon as you plant, swing the leg forward, snapping both the knee joint and the hip joint forward. Keep your toe pointed down and whack the ball with your instep. Try to hit the ball in the center; if you hit it a little off to the side, it will spin.

Keep your knee over the ball in order to keep the ball on the ground.

There are times, however, when you want that ball up in the air. You'll use the instep pass for this—not the toes!—but your approach will be slightly different. Place your plant foot a good distance back from the ball, about 10 inches, rather than next to it. Then, lean back a little when you contact the ball. Remember, if your knee is over the ball, the ball will stay on the ground. If you have your knee back from the ball, the ball will rise into the air. Also, try to contact the ball on its lower half. This will also help lift it.

The pass on the ground is easier for your teammates to control, but there are times when the lofted pass comes in handy. It's used mainly to get over the heads of defenders. If you see a player who is wide open across the field, you can loft the ball over to her, bypassing the defenders. A lofted pass is also used for free kicks—such as corner kicks, goal kicks, direct kicks, and indirect kicks—when defenders set up to block everything else.

Passing Strategy

Now take this short true-false quiz to find out what you know about passing strategy.

1. You should never pass the ball backward.
2. If the ball has spent a long time on one side of the field, it's a good idea to switch it to the other side.
3. It's always better to pass than to dribble.
4. A pass is an easy way to get around a defender.
5. The only lofted passes are long balls.

And now here are the answers. Let's see how you did.

Tip

Many soccer players find it easier to lift the ball if they approach it from an angle.

Just for Fun

A good game to play using your short ball-passing skills is Hot Potato. You'll probably need at least four players, one ball, and a timer. Set the timer and start passing the ball around your circle. Whoever ends up with the ball when the timer goes off is out. Another way to play is that, instead of being out, she gets a letter in the word POTATO each time she's caught with the ball. In other words, the first time, she gets a P, the second time, an O, and so on. That way, it takes six turns to be eliminated. This game is great for working on your accuracy and your speed in passing.

Just for Fun

Now that you've learned all the different passes, it's time to play a game. You're your friends, find a field somewhere, and split up into two equal teams. You use one ball, but you don't need any goals. To get a point, a team has to get six passes in a row, without the other team touching the ball. Set a limit such as five points or twenty minutes of play, so that you know when the game is over.

wall pass: Also called the give-and-go or the 1–2 pass, it is a way of getting around a defender by "bouncing" the ball off one of your teammates. Your teammate receives the ball while you run around the defender and then passes it back to you when you're free.

1. *False.* Passing backward is a great strategic move. If you're having trouble moving the ball forward, back up and try again. Maybe a different route will work. It's better to take a little longer and hold on to the ball, than push it up quickly and lose possession.

2. *True.* If a ball has been on one side for a long time, there's a good chance that the defense has been pulled over. If you can switch the ball to the other side of the field, with a long lofted pass, for instance, then you might find a teammate who has no one guarding him.

3. *False.* If no one is moving in to defend against you, take a few dribbles. If no one is on you, then that means ten of the other team's players are guarding only nine of yours. That's not the best situation to start passing the ball. Take what they'll give you. If they'll let you dribble all the way to the goal, then take a shot, too. Don't forget, though, once they do commit and move in to defend, you need to get rid of the ball quickly. Look to pass it off to the person who was left open by that move.

4. *True.* If you see a wide-open field in front of you with only one defender between you and the goal, then a **wall pass** is the perfect thing to use. Call "wall" to one of your teammates and pass the ball off to her. Run around the defender and your teammate should pass the ball back to you. If your defender stays with you, your teammate can take the ball to the goal herself. But more likely the defender will follow the ball, which leaves you open for a nice pass back. That's why it's called a wall pass. Your teammate has acted like a wall that you can bounce the ball off, then receive it, and go on.

The wall pass

5. *False.* Occasionally you might want to loft the ball over the opponent's head without it going too far. This is called a **chip.** Essentially you want to use the same motion as a lofted pass, getting your instep under the ball and leaning backward, but you don't want to follow through. Make your kick a sharp stab at the ball rather than a smooth kick. This should give it some air and some backspin but not much distance.

Scoring a Goal

A ball lofted into the upper right corner goal. A bullet drilled to the far left of the goalie. A diving header off a corner kick. A nudge with the outside of the foot, catching the keeper out of

Just for Fun

One good passing game for four players is called Double Jeopardy. Have two players line up on one line and two others stand across from them at a good passing distance for your level. Use two balls, one on each side. Now start passing the ball back and forth. The team who can get both balls on one side is the winner.

Just for Fun

Knockout is a great game to practice your shooting. It's especially good for practice volleys. Find a wall and mark off a goal area. You and your friends line up in a single line in front of it. The first person takes a shot at the goal. The next person must get the rebound and one-touch it back into the goal, and so on. When a person misses, he's knocked out. The last one left is the winner.

Tip

If your kick is strong enough to get it into the goal from the 18-yard line, then use that marking to remind yourself that you should take the shot.

position. A dribbler rolling past the goalkeeper's fingertips. All of these are goals; all are equal no matter how spectacular or unspectacular they look; and all will make you a hero with your teammates. Officially, a goal is when the ball crosses fully over the goal line, between the two goalposts.

Most of your shots should be taken with your instep. This will give you the most powerful kick. When you're passing, you have to be worried about sending the ball to your teammate at a speed he can handle. When you're shooting, the last thing you want is for the goalkeeper to be able to handle it.

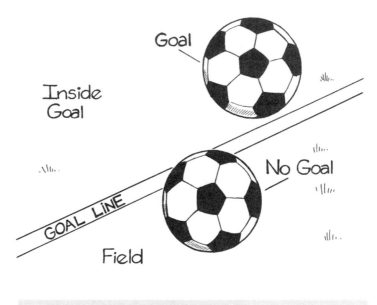

Official goal

The Volley

When you're in front of the goal, you're not going to be given much time to settle the ball in front of you, get control, and get off a nice, sweet shot. Many shots will be taken with your head. Other shots will still be in the air but at a level where you can use your foot. These are called **volleys**, or **half-volleys** if you get them off the bounce.

To kick a volley, you'll want to use your instep. Lean forward over the ball to keep it low, and keep your eye on the ball. Make sure you use your arms to keep your balance since you'll be taking the shot on one leg. Because the ball is coming at you with some force already, this shot will be quite powerful.

> **WORDS to KNOW**
>
> **volley:** A shot in which the player kicks the ball out of the air.
>
> **half-volley:** A shot in which the player kicks the ball immediately after it has bounced. The ball is still in the air but only a bit off the ground.

The Slider

If the ball is near the goal line and just needs a nudge in the right direction, the slider shot might be your best bet. Take a running start and slide into the ball, much as a baseball player would slide into home plate. Chances are there will be a defender right on that ball trying to get it out of there, so you need to make sure to get your foot on the ball, not on the defender. You have to touch the ball first or you'll be called for tripping.

Teamwork

It takes two players to make a successful pass. And it takes two halves to make a successful compound word! Listed below are two sets of three-letter words. First unscramble the words in column A. Then, match each word in column A with a word in column B to form a new word. We've done the first one for you.

A	B	
~~YEE~~	BID	EYELID
ORF	ROT	_____
NPA	AGE	_____
ONT	FIT	_____
RAC	TRY	_____
OTC	~~LID~~	_____
AMN	ICE	_____
UTO	TON	_____

HINT: The word in column A should always come first.

Just for Fun

A good way to practice shooting for the sides of the goal is to place two cones about 3 feet in from each of the goalposts. Now play your regular soccer game, but the only goal that counts is the ball that goes between a cone and a goalpost. Anything that goes between the two cones is not a goal.

Shooting Strategy

You can't get the ball into the goal if you don't take the shot. That may sound obvious, but too many players goof around in front of the goal, waiting for the perfect shot. I've got news for you. It's not going to come. The defenders are not going to back off and let you line up your shot perfectly. Just get in there and shoot the ball. And don't pass it off to your teammate because he has a better kick or a stronger foot, unless he has a better angle. If you find yourself within shooting distance of the goal, go for it. And you're going to have to be able to use either foot, because you won't have time to set the ball up in front of your stronger foot. So be sure to practice with both feet.

And while we're giving rather obvious advice, here's another tip that many soccer players need to hear: Don't kick it to the keeper. Believe it or not, players tend to go for the middle of the goal, right where the goalkeeper is. Maybe this is because she is a nice neat target, or maybe shooters feel that if they go for the corners, they might miss the goal completely. Who knows? But when you're shooting, aim for the edges.

While you're shooting for the corner of the goal, also pay attention to the size of your goalkeeper. If you're playing against a very short keeper in a regulation-size goal, then a lofted ball is going to be successful. If you're older and your opponent's keeper is almost the size of an adult, then send the ball low. It's going to be a lot harder for him to bend down or dive than to stay standing up to block the ball.

And finally, the best tip of all: Follow your shot. As soon as you take your shot, charge into the goal. Even if you end up kicking it straight to the keeper, there's a good chance that it will be too hard for her to handle on her first touch. Any sort of rebound from her hand, a defender, or the goalpost is another opportunity for you to put it in the goal.

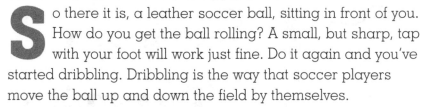

Why couldn't the soccer player make a phone call?

She couldn't find a receiver!

Just for Fun

Red Light, Green Light has always been a great kids' game and it can be played with a soccer ball as well. One person is the "traffic light" at the far end of the field. The rest are the "cars." They each have a ball. The player at the far end yells, "Green light!" and turns around. The cars all begin dribbling their balls until they hear the traffic light yell, "Red light!" at which point they all must put a foot on the ball. If any players can't put their foot on the ball because it's too far away from them, then they're sent back to the beginning. The winner (and next traffic light) is the player who crosses the field first. This really teaches you to keep the ball close yet still dribble quickly.

So there it is, a leather soccer ball, sitting in front of you. How do you get the ball rolling? A small, but sharp, tap with your foot will work just fine. Do it again and you've started dribbling. Dribbling is the way that soccer players move the ball up and down the field by themselves.

Can you guess how many parts of the foot soccer players use? If you guessed four, you're right! Soccer players use the inside of their feet, the outside of their feet, the bottom of their feet, and the top of their feet. The top is the area where your shoelaces are, and it's called the instep. But what about the toes, you ask? The toes are kind of like knees. It's legal to use them, but you won't get much control.

Start Simple

You can practice dribbling anywhere: on a field, in the park, your backyard, or even inside if you're allowed. To start, put the ball on the ground and move it forward. Try to get from one end of your playing area to the other. Be sure to use every part of both feet. The more ways you know how to dribble, the more options you have when you're trying to get away from a defender.

Once you feel comfortable moving the ball around the field, you can make it more interesting and turn yourself into a whiz-bang dribbler by trying some of these variations:

1. Dribble only with your left foot and then only with your right. Then dribble alternating between the two feet every time.
2. Dribble only with the inside of your foot. Then dribble with only the outside. Then just use your instep. Try alternating between those three.

3. Make your course curvy instead of a straight line. Pretend that the trees and bushes are defenders that you have to avoid. Use sweatshirts or leaves or anything else if you're playing in a place without trees.

4. Place your hand under your eyes to block your vision of the ball. Now try to dribble through your course. The best players are able to look up and see what the field situation is like. They can't be watching the ball the whole time.

5. Time yourself. Set up a course and see how fast you can get through it. Don't do this in a wide-open field, however, because all you'll end up doing is kicking it much too far ahead. You want to practice speed in an area where you still need to control the ball and keep it close to your feet.

6. Turn some of these dribbling exercises into a race.

Practice dribbling whenever you get a chance. You don't need much space and you don't need anyone else to do it with you. The more chances your feet get to touch the ball, the more comfortable they will be when you're out on the field and the more you'll understand just which way the ball is going to roll.

Tip

The closer you keep the ball to your feet, the more control you'll have.

Fancy Footwork

Once you've mastered the straight dribble, it's time to add to your bag of tricks. And "tricks" is the right word! You want to use your dribbling to fool the defenders. There won't be many teams that will let you take the ball from one end of the field to the other without trying to stop you. So what can you do?

If a defender is closing in on you quickly, the first thing you're going to want to do is look to pass the ball off to

Why are soccer balls black and white?

Because if they were red (read) all over they'd be a newspaper!

WORDS to KNOW

shielding: The process of keeping your body between the defender and the ball to prevent the defender from getting to the ball.

someone who is open, but sometimes, you don't have that option. It's all up to you. There are three options for you: protect the ball (also called shielding), turn, or fake.

Shielding

Protecting the ball is easiest and safest of the three options. You put your body between the ball and the defender and continue dribbling, keeping the ball very close to your feet but as far away from the opponent as possible.

Tip

When you are shielding the ball, remember that your arms are off-limits. Not only can't you use them to touch the ball, but you also can't use them to keep your opponent back. Use your body to block him from the ball. Use your arms for balance, not to push your opponent away.

Shielding the ball

This is also called **shielding** the ball. You are acting like a protective shield placed between the defender and the ball.

It takes quite a bit of skill to shield the ball for a long time. Look and listen for a teammate who has come to help you. You can also try to escape by making a strong fake move with your body in one direction. If the defender goes for it, then take off in the other direction.

Practice, Practice, Practice

First, read this advice from Michelle Akers, a U.S. Women's World Cup player. She says, "My suggestion is to use your [weaker foot] as much as possible. That means use it all the time, every time, for everything you do on the soccer field. Use it in warm-up, for dribbling, shooting, receiving, in drills, when you train extra, etc. Whatever you are doing, use only your [weak] foot."

Now, figure out where to put each of the scrambled letters in the following puzzle. They all fit in spaces under their own column. When you have filled in the grid, you will be able to see what Michelle Akers promises this practicing will help you to do!

```
B F     T   O     T I E   S O C   E     P U     3
I E S Y N D A F G H T E   S O U C R   Y O O A E I Y
D H E A U T D O O H E D S F G N A A A N T E L Y B L L
T A Y   E S W R F I T T H S I M O R T H R W H L E W E R O
```

Turning

Turning is a little harder. A turn means that you are heading down the field in one direction; then you quickly stop the ball, turn, and dribble off in the other direction. Most of the time this means you're heading back toward your own goal, but this isn't a problem. If the turn let you escape from the defender, you're in good shape. Now you have a second or two to look up and find a teammate who is looking for a pass.

Turns work best when the defender is running alongside you, going in the same direction. That way her momentum will be carrying her forward and it will take her a second to recover and go in the other direction, especially if you catch her by surprise.

Tip

If a player isn't fooled by your turn, try another one immediately. So now you've turned 360 degrees, and you're heading right back in the direction you started.

Here are some of the most popular turns:

The drag back: This is where the bottom of your foot comes into play. You step on top of the ball and pull it back behind you. Spin 180 degrees and take off.

The drag back

The inside turn: Step over the ball and using the inside of your foot, push the ball back in the other direction.

The inside of the foot turn

The outside turn: For this one, you'll want to nudge the ball backward with the outside of your foot, again turning your body 180 degrees and following the ball.

The outside of the foot turn

The box turn: This is similar to the inside turn, but you push the ball under your body before you turn your body. Make an L-shape with your two feet and push the ball under your body. Then spin and take off in the other direction.

Speed is the key to a great turn. You want to catch the defender by surprise when you are both running quickly in the same direction. You know when you're going to make the turn, so your body is prepared to slow down and go the other way. But the defender has no idea. He is going to need an extra second to do all that, and that's when you lose him. If the two of you are not moving quickly, then the defender will find it much easier to stop and turn with you. And if you don't make your turn quickly, then he'll find it easy to catch up with you, too.

Fakes

But what if the defender is coming full speed right at you? Turning and running in the opposite direction might sound really appealing, but it's not your best option. This is the time for a fake. A fake basically means that you're going to try to make the opponent think that you're going in one direction when you really plan to move in the other direction. There are a whole bunch of different fakes, but all of them have a few things in common. You have to:

- Be fast
- Use your whole body
- Be convincing
- Stay low

No matter what fake you try, you aren't going to fool anyone if you don't do those four things.

The first one is obvious. If you're trying to fake someone out, you have to be fast. If you take too long, then even if you do fool the other player at first, he's going to have plenty of time to recover.

The second tip is important, too. You might not realize it, but you generally move your whole body when you change directions or make a move. Many players give themselves away when they only fake with their legs. The defender can tell that you're really not going that way because it doesn't look natural. Or in other words, your fake looks fake. So make sure you get your whole body involved.

Third, be convincing. In general, this tip should follow naturally if you're concentrating on the first two tips. If you're moving quickly and using your whole body, you'll most likely look as though you're going the way you're faking. Just make

Tip

When you turn around after doing a drag back, turn toward the leg that pulled the ball back. That way you see the ball the whole time you're turning.

Just for Fun

To see how well a turn works, you and a friend should try it without a ball. Find a good starting point, like a tree or a fence. The idea is to have a race, away from the tree and then back to it. But your friend isn't going to know how far out you plan to go. Say ready, set, go, and then you both start sprinting away from it in one direction. Suddenly, turn around and sprint back to the starting place. I'll bet you beat your friend. Now let her be the one who turns. This time, she'll beat you.

Just for Fun

You'll be able to practice a ton of shielding, turning, and faking if you play a little one-on-one with a friend. Set up two goals—they can be as simple as a T-shirt on the ground that you have to hit—and then try to score.

Jokin' Around

Why do soccer players have terrible table manners?
Because they're always dribbling.

sure that your fake is significant enough to be noticed. Make a hard shift to the left or right, not just a slight lean.

And finally, stay low and keep your knees bent. It's going to be hard to keep your balance with all that shifting back and forth. You want to get the opponent off balance, not yourself.

Here are some common fakes:

The step-over: Swing your leg as though you're going to pass or shoot the ball, but instead lift it a little higher and step over the ball. Then push the ball in the opposite direction with the outside of your foot.

The step-over

The shimmy: Shift your whole body in one direction without lifting your feet off the ground. Then kick the ball in the other direction.

The stop and start: For this move, you want to dribble hard in one direction and then stop the ball as if you're going to switch directions. As soon as the defender moves to block you, continue in the same direction.

Smart Moves

Now that you know all the great moves, you probably want to know some strategy. When are you supposed to dribble instead of passing or shooting? There are a few smart guidelines.

First of all, if you're all by yourself and no one is challenging you, go ahead and dribble. Take as much of the field as the defenders will give you. I can't imagine that any team would let you take the ball from one end of the field to the other, but until they send someone in to stop you, give it a try.

When they do approach you, however, it's time to rethink. If there's an open player nearby, you can send the ball to her. She can then pass it back to you for the easy wall pass that you learned about in Chapter 3. This is a much better, almost fool-proof, option than trying to dribble around the defender.

You also don't want to be dribbling when you're in front of your goal. That's a really dangerous area to be fooling around in. Instead, get the ball out of there! Use a series of short passes or one long kick, but clear it out of the goal area. Don't rely on any fancy footwork, because you could easily get burned.

You might think that if you're in front of the other team's goal, the advice would be just the opposite, but that's not the case. You don't want to dribble there, either. This time, though, forget passing. Shoot! Dribble if you need to get clear to take a shot, but if you're inside that box, boot the ball into the goal.

So, to put it simply:

Goal areas = no dribbling

Finally, you don't want to dribble if there's someone else wide open and closer to the goal. Even if you're a fast runner, you're not going to be faster than a good hard pass.

Tip

Just because you see a defender approaching doesn't mean that you should immediately pass the ball. Wait until he actually commits to challenging you. Otherwise you'll make it easy for him to intercept your pass.

Online Kick

Soccer America is a magazine that will keep you up-to-date on all the soccer issues in this country. You'll find a lot of it on line at *www.socceramerica.com.*

Keep Your Eye on the Ball

All thirteen of the words in this puzzle can be followed by the word BALL. See how many words you can figure out and fit into the criss-cross grid. HINT: We've left you the first letter of each!

Soccer   Wiffle   Basket
Base   Ping pong   Snow
Foot   Tee   Bowling
Golf   Tether
Tennis   Dodge

Preki

One of the best dribblers in the game is a Yugoslavian-born soccer star named Preki. His feet move so fast that you can't even be sure what move he's making. He helped the Kansas City Wizards win the MLS (Major League Soccer) Cup in 2000 and currently plays for the Miami Fusion. The MLS is the professional men's soccer league in the United States. Even though he was born in Yugoslavia, Preki became a U.S. citizen in 1996. This made him a very valuable addition to the U.S. team in the 1998 World Cup competition.

So send the ball down the field to your teammate and race to support her. The key to remember in this situation is that your teammate has to be "wide open." Just because your teammate is closer to the goal doesn't mean that she's able to receive a pass. This is especially true if no one is guarding you. Think about it. If no one is on you, the other team has ten of their players guarding the other nine players on your team. You might just want to keep the ball and start tap, tap, tapping your way toward the goal.

Goalkeeper, keeper, goaltender, goalie, handman, netminder—there are tons of different names for the person who stands in front of the big net known as the goal (lunatic is another). And that player has even more responsibilities than he or she has names.

In fact, the goalkeeper is so important that the position is set apart from the rest of the positions in three ways: the goalkeeper wears a different uniform, he gets to use his hands, and she gets her own chapter in this book.

Clothes

The goalkeeper has the greatest uniform. It doesn't have to match anything. In fact, it must be a different color from the shirts of the field players on both teams. Sometimes, it's just a bright color, but many goalies today love to wear something a little wilder, with swirls or tie-dye designs or even a bull's-eye.

There are three reasons behind the keeper's wild shirt. The first and most important reason is that the referee has to be able to distinguish between a regular field player and the goalie. The ref must know in an instant whether the person touching the ball with his hand is the one who is allowed to do so.

Second, the wilder the shirt, the less likely it is to match the shirts of the other team. If a player just has a royal blue jersey, for instance, she'll have to come up with a different shirt when her team plays a team whose shirts are royal blue.

The last reason doesn't have anything to do with the rules, but it has a lot to do with a player's brain. Studies have shown that players focus on the keeper's bright shirt and tend to kick it right to him. The mass of color in the center of the goal just attracts their eyes. That's why the more outrageous the shirt is, the better. Design your own goalie shirt here. What would you like to wear?

A goalie shirt to draw on

Because the goalkeeper can't rely on everyone kicking the ball to her just because she's wearing a wild shirt, she also has to rely on her ability to catch or stop the ball from going into the goal. Helping her do this are a pair of goalie gloves. Almost all goalkeepers above a certain level wear gloves. Gloves give the keeper a much better grip on the ball. Some are simple gloves with a piece of rubber sewn into the palm and finger areas, but some are way more elaborate and must be wet down before the game to create a super grip on the ball.

The rest of the outfit isn't as important. Many keepers like to wear padded shorts. These shorts have cushions in the hip area, so if the keeper has to dive to save the ball, it won't hurt so much when he hits the ground. Cleats, socks, and shin guards make up the rest of the goalie gear.

Uniform Uniforms

Oops—goalies are supposed to wear shirts that are different from the rest of the team. These goalies look too much the same! Cross out the three pairs of goalies who are wearing exactly the same shirts. Circle the one goalie who has a shirt that is different from everyone else's. This goalie will get to play today!

Keeping to the Rules

Now the keeper is dressed to kill—or at least block, stop, and save—so it's time to get in the goal. The rules say that the keeper is allowed to use her hands when she's inside the box marked off at 18 yards. She is allowed to come out of that box, but while she's outside, she can only use her feet. The other time that she is required to use her feet is when a ball is passed back to her from one of her teammates. The keeper used to be allowed to pick up the ball, but players were using this option so often that it made the game a little boring. Forcing the keeper to use her feet on a pass back has reduced this play considerably. In fact, passing back to the keeper can be risky at younger levels of play. But as defenders and keepers become more comfortable with each other and as their skills improve, passing back to the keeper can be a smart way to restart the whole play and allow the defense to settle.

Once the keeper has the ball in her hands, she has six seconds to get rid of it. Most keepers like to run to the front of the box before throwing or kicking the ball to their teammates, because it allows them to gain a little more ground. But they need to do it quickly. If they take longer than six seconds, the other team gets an indirect kick. Once the goalkeeper has released the ball, she cannot touch it again until someone else has touched it.

Play Catch

Catching the ball is not quite as simple as it sounds. Sure you have the fancy gloves and you've been catching balls since you were in preschool, but the goalie catch has a few more

skills involved. Circle the body parts that you think will help you catch the ball.

Elbows	Head
Hands	Knees
Eyes	Legs
Feet	Hips
Fingers	Torso

Okay, that was an easy one. It's all of them. Use everything you've got to keep the ball from getting into the goal, but keep in mind that all those other body parts are there to help your hands. Don't make the mistake some young players do of using your feet to kick the ball away when you have the opportunity to pick up the ball.

The best way to catch a ball depends on how the ball is coming toward you. Let's say it's rolling on the ground. To pick up a rolling ball, there are five basic steps:

1. Move your body behind the ball.
2. Go down on one knee.
3. Lean forward.
4. Scoop the ball into your chest.
5. Stand up.

The reasons behind the first three moves are the same. You're guarding against a miss. If you have your body behind the ball, it acts as a wall. If you get down on one knee, the ball can't go through your legs. If you're leaning forward and the ball bounces out of your hands, then your body knocks it back down and you can dive on it.

> **Tip**
>
> Don't get lazy and neglect to go down on your knee if the ball is a slow easy roller. You never know when the ball will hit a bump in the field and pop up. You want your body there to block it.

Down on the knee to pick up a ground shot

If the ball is coming in the air, you want a very different kind of catch. The first step is the same, however. Get your body behind the ball. You need all the help you can to block the ball from going into the goal. Now, however, instead of scooping up the ball, you want your hands out, palms forward rather than facing up. Keep them close together so that your pointer fingers and your thumbs form a W.

Keep your elbows bent so when you catch the ball, your hands can move back into your chest, taking away some of the impact of the shot. As soon as you've caught the ball, swing your hands around and hug it to your chest.

Those are the easy catches. Unfortunately, there are going to be lots of times when it's going to take all you've got just to get your fingers over to the ball, much less your whole body. Here are some tips to help you deal with those difficult balls.

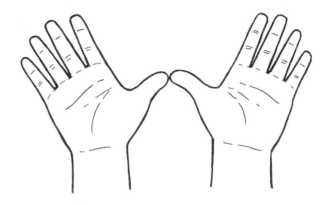

Forming a W with the thumb and forefingers

Tip

All goalkeepers should spend time playing in the field as well as in the goal so they'll have a better idea of what their field players can do. It also keeps their foot skills sharp.

- If you have to jump for a ball, go off of one leg. It will get you more height.
- If you are unsure about being able to grab the ball, tip it over the top or off to the side of the goal. If you play wait-and-see, you'll probably end up tipping it into the goal if you can't catch it.
- If an opponent is coming in to head the ball at the same time you are trying to catch it, punch the ball away. Your hands can reach higher than her head, but you won't necessarily have the strength to pull the ball into your chest. You can't risk a loose ball in front of the goal, so reach up and punch it out with your fist or fists.
- If a ball is coming in hard on the ground and you aren't going to be able to go down on one knee to save it, dive. This way your body will act as a barrier.

Cutting the Angle

You can cut down on the number of risky saves by paying attention to where you and the shooter are in relation to the goal. If the shooter is coming in from the side, you should move over a little to that side. See what that does to her possible shots.

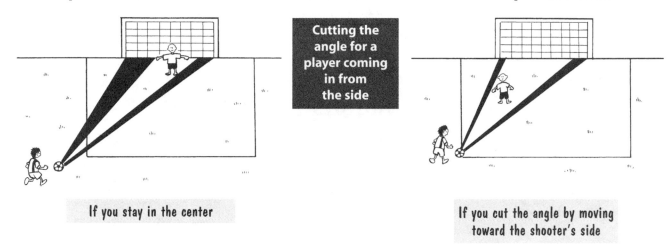

Cutting the angle for a player coming in from the side

If you stay in the center

If you cut the angle by moving toward the shooter's side

If it's a one-on-one breakaway situation, face it: You're in big trouble. But there are a couple of things you can do that are a little more effective than crossing your fingers for luck. The first thing you should do is move slowly toward the dribbling player. Look what happens to the available goal area when you move forward.

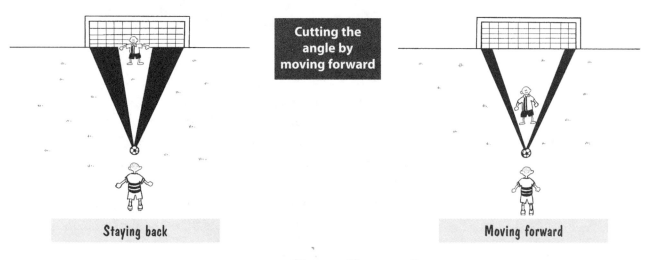

Cutting the angle by moving forward

Staying back

Moving forward

But *slowly* is the key word here. You don't want to rush out and have the dribbler fake around you to an open goal. And you don't want him to make an easy chip over your head either. But if you move out slowly, he may feel forced to take a shot at a considerably smaller goal area, or he may make a mistake. If you notice that he's dribbled slightly too far out in front of himself and you think you can get the ball, go for it.

Getting Rid of the Ball

Okay, you've made your spectacular save. The ball is gripped tightly in between your state-of-the-art gloves. And you have only six seconds to do something with it. What do you do? First, look to see if you have someone wide open, who is breaking away and who could benefit from a quick release. If that's the case, immediately get the ball to that player. If not, which is most of the time, run out to the 18-yard line. Why waste 16 feet of your punt or throw by standing back in the goal?

Once you're out at the 18, you have three choices:

- Kick
- Throw
- Roll

The kick will get the ball farthest down the field. You want to use this when the opponents haven't gotten back quickly and you might gain an advantage down at their end. You also want to use this when the opponents are dominating you. The ball has spent way too much time in your end. Get it out of there.

You can use any kind of kick that works best for you, but most goaltenders find that the punt gets them the most distance. To

Speed Drill

This tiny picture puzzle shows where the goalie is allowed to use her hands. Where is that?

Tip

No matter when you're taking a big kick—whether it's a corner kick, a goal kick, or a punt (but especially with a punt)—keep your head still and your eye on the ball the whole time.

punt, hold the ball in both hands out in front of your body. Take a hop to plant your non-kicking foot and drop the ball. Your kicking foot should then swing forward and connect with the underside of the ball just before it hits the ground. Follow through with your leg in the direction you want the ball to go.

The downside of using the punt is that it's not as accurate. If you need accuracy more than distance, use a roll or a throw. Use the roll when you have a player fairly near you who has no chance of being intercepted. Give the ball a hard underhanded roll in the direction of your teammate. A roll is nice because it's on the ground and therefore easy to handle.

But let's say there are opponents milling around. You don't want to roll the ball out because if an opponent gets hold of it, it's coming right back at you in seconds. In this case, the throw is the best option. It gives you much more distance and allows you to get the ball over the head of your opponents.

Your teammates should be breaking out toward the touchlines (or sidelines) as soon as you save the ball. Look there for one of them to be open. You should never throw the ball up the middle. It's much too dangerous. Throwing the ball up the side gives you a little more time to recover if the opponents manage to steal the ball.

To make the throw, take one arm back with the ball in that hand. Point the other arm at your target. Take a step with the leg opposite your throwing arm and swing your throwing arm in a wide arc out toward your teammate. As that arm goes up, your outstretched pointing arm should come down. Your hips will twist forward, with your body coming forward after them. Snap your wrist at the last minute as you let go of the ball.

Tip

The bigger the arc you make with your arms when throwing the ball, the farther it will go.

The goalkeeper throw

Communication

← GOALKEEPER

The goaltender should be the director on the field. No one can see the entire game as well as you can, and you need to open your big mouth and tell people what you see. If a teammate has time to get the ball under control, yell "time!" If he needs to get rid of it immediately, yell, "one touch!" or "man on!" or whatever other term your team uses. Tell your defense to push up if they're hanging back. Call a defender off if you think you can get the ball first. It's much better for the goalkeeper to have the ball under control than for a defender to merely be clearing it out of the goal area.

When the referee calls a direct kick against your team and the ball is down near the goal

The wall

area, your team will want to set up a wall. This is when your direction is most important. You'll learn more about the field player's role in the wall in the chapter on defensive strategies. As a

We're with You!

This team is really supporting their keeper! Using a simple number substitution code (A=1, B=2, etc.) figure out what the team is spelling out with the numbers on their jerseys.

keeper, you must know how to line the field players up. Take the last player on the wall and line her up with the post, yet 10 feet from the ball. Every other player should be shoulder to shoulder with that first player. You take the space on the far side of the goal that's left open. If the other team does chip it over the wall, it will be a slow backspin ball, which should give you the time you need to move over.

Never Blame the Keeper

Most important, don't blame yourself if you let one in. One thing you need to learn before you become a goalkeeper, and one thing that every soccer player should learn before they take the field, is that the goalkeeper cannot be blamed for the loss. The keeper is the last line of defense. He's there to save the team from all their mistakes. Think about it. When you start the game, the ball is in the center of the field and there are ten players on your team between the ball and the goal. It is only after all ten of you fail to gain possession of the ball and move it in the other direction that the goalkeeper gets his hands on it. Okay, who's to blame then?

> Which goalie can jump higher than the cage?
>
> All of them can, because the cage can't jump!

Brianna Scurry

Brianna Scurry is a player on the Atlanta Beat, but she rose to fame as the goalkeeper for the 1999 Women's World Cup Championship team. During that exciting competition, Brianna played every minute of every game. She had only four goals scored against her and had three shutouts in the match. In the final game, against China, she saved one of the shootout penalty kicks to give the U.S. women the victory and the World Cup!

WORDS to KNOW

WUSA: The Women's United Soccer Association. The WUSA is the professional women's soccer league in the United States.

 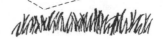
Some of the best goalkeeping performances have come from keepers on lousy teams. If a keeper gets fifty shots on goal and saves forty-eight of them, that's impressive. If her team is able to get only four shots off at the other end and the goalie saves all four, then the score is still a 2–0 loss. But who put in the better goalkeeping performance? I think it was the keeper who saved forty-eight shots instead of only four.

Listen to your goalkeeper, respect your goalkeeper, and do whatever you can to keep the ball away from your goalkeeper.

Just for Fun

It's hard to get used to the idea of throwing yourself on the ground for a diving save. To work up to it, try this with a friend. Kneel on the ground and have your friend throw the ball to one side or the other. Fall on your side as you grab the ball. You'll notice it really doesn't hurt that much. Once you get used to the motion of catching the ball as you fall on your side, you'll have an easier time of diving for it.

Jose Luis Chilavert

Jose Luis Chilavert is the goalkeeper for the Paraguay national team. Aside from being the best goalkeeper in his country, Jose has another claim to fame. He holds the world record for goal scoring by a goalkeeper. He's scored forty-four of them! He takes the penalty kicks and many direct and indirect kicks for his team. He's also the only goalkeeper to ever score in a World Cup match and the only one to ever have scored twice in one game.

Chapter 6

On the Attack

Just for Fun

A version of Monkey in the Middle called Coneball is a fun way to practice your passing and off-the-ball movement skills. Place a cone in the center of your area. If you have three or four players, have one defender. If you have five, six, or seven players, increase it to two defenders, and so on. For the example, let's do a five-on-two situation. The object of the game is to see if the five players on the outside can hit the cone with the ball. The two defenders try to stop them, but they're not allowed within 3 feet of the cone. The outside players pass the ball around until they get an open shot.

Tip

On the kickoff, sometimes the best strategy is to pass back, just to ensure you remain in possession of the ball.

Ever hear the expression "Possession is nine-tenths of the law"? Well, even if you haven't, remember it now because possession is nine-tenths of soccer strategy. If you have the ball, you want to keep it. If your team can hold on to the ball, then the other team can't shoot. And if they can't shoot, they can't score. Pretty simple.

The hard part comes when you try to figure out how to hold on to that ball once you've got it.

Pass, Pass, Pass

Soccer is a team sport, so be sure to play the game that way. If you constantly pass the ball back and forth between your teammates, the defense is going to have a hard time getting ahold of the ball. It's like a giant game of Monkey in the Middle. They'll be running around like chickens with their heads cut off, and you'll be setting yourselves up for a shot on goal. At least that is what we'd like to happen.

But just because passing is the best offensive strategy, that doesn't mean that you should pass every time you get the ball. If they're giving you the space to dribble, take it. Force them to commit to guarding you, and you'll be more likely to find someone else open for a pass.

And that brings us to another key point of passing. The receiver is just as important as the passer. A receiver might be wide open on the touchlines, but he's completely use-less to the passer if there are a couple of defenders between them. Moving when you don't have the ball is just as important as when you have the ball. Run to a spot that's open and in a good line to receive a pass.

One of the key aspects to good passing is having receivers who stay spread out. That way you create some open spaces

in the middle to run into. For some reason, the ball is like a magnet to most young players. If you watch a game played by kindergartners, it looks like a swarm of bees has gathered around the ball to move it down the field. It's hard to pass if your teammate is 6 inches away. One concept that I think is helpful is to think of the field like a big sailboat. If everyone runs to one side of the boat it's going to tip over. You need to keep the boat balanced for smooth sailing.

Tip

Know what your teammates can do. If the player with the ball can't kick it more than 20 feet, don't stand 40 feet away and call for the ball.

Knowing Your Position

At the start of each game, the coach will give each player a position. Knowing what is expected of each position will help you stay spread out once the game starts. Coaches use a variety of formations, but the positions can be broken down in three basic categories: forwards, midfielders, and defenders.

Here are two of the many possible formations:

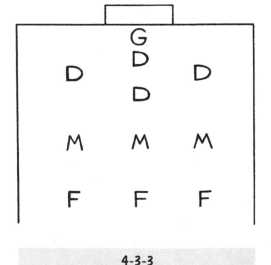

4-3-3

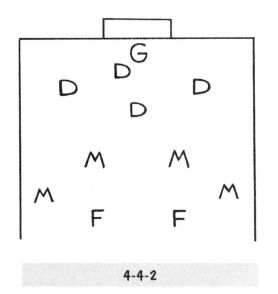

4-4-2

In general, the forwards are always in front of the midfielders who are in front of the defenders. Sometimes a player will make an overlapping run if he sees an opportunity, but it's usually a good idea to hold your position. For instance, if a forward is always hanging back with the defenders, then there's no one to receive the ball when it gets into the opponent's half of the field. And if defenders are always running up trying to score, then there is very little protecting the goal. If you're a player who likes to run all over, then perhaps you should think about playing midfield. While the midfielders generally stay in between the defenders and the forwards, they are expected to go all the way up for the attack and all the way back to defend.

No matter where you play, you should realize that all ten field players are responsible for shooting, passing, and defending. When your team has the ball, everyone is on the attack. When the other team has the ball, everyone is on defense.

Tip

Meet the ball! Let's say you've made a great run into an open space and your teammate passes you the ball. Do you wait for it to come to you? Absolutely not! Go get it.

wing: Sometimes coaches will refer to a forward as a wing or a striker. The wings play out near the touchline, while the striker is another term for the center forward.

striker: Another term for the center forward.

Spread the Defense

It's also important to be aware of your positioning side to side. If you're on the left side, try not to drift into the middle or even worse, over to the right. In other words, don't tip the boat. Holding your position not only opens up passing opportunities as we discussed earlier, but it helps to spread the defense. If you and your teammates are all spread out, one of two things has to happen.

1. The defense stays bunched up in the middle protecting their goal, which means you're free to dribble down the side.
2. The defense comes out to the touchline to challenge you, which means they leave a lot of field space open in the middle. In that case, you and your teammates can make runs through the open middle to receive the ball.

Spreading the defense

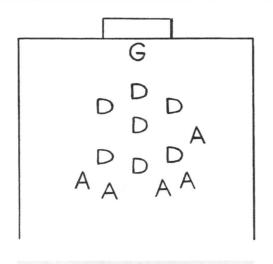

Tightly bunched

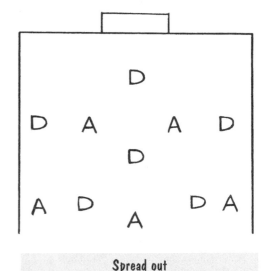

Spread out

The drawback of going wide is that the defenders are going to try to trap you in the corner. You'll need to make a move to the middle well before you get there. Although it's nice to be able to have some space along the touchlines to dribble, you need to get the ball into the middle in order to score. If you see an opportunity at any time, once you've passed the centerline, you need to go for it. Your teammate can always bring it back out to the side if he finds it too congested in the middle. A zigzag pattern down the field is quite effective.

One of the best ways to get the ball into the center is a **cross**. If you find yourself a step ahead of the defender, turn in toward the goal and send a high lofted pass to one of your teammates who should be waiting for the cross in front of the goal. The ideal cross should come down in front of the goal right in the vicinity of your teammate's head. Then he can put his forehead on it and redirect it into the goal.

WORDS to KNOW

cross: A high lofted pass into the center of the field in front of the goal. The ideal cross should come down in the vicinity of a teammate's head. Then he can put his forehead on it and redirect it into the goal.

Spreading the defense will work even right in front of the goal. If your teammate is bringing the ball up the middle, don't stand in the middle waiting for him to pass to you. Start running out to the edge of the box. If a defender doesn't follow you, then you're wide open for a pass and then a shot. If he does, then you've cleared out the middle for your teammate with the ball. Either way, there's a good chance you'll get a shot off.

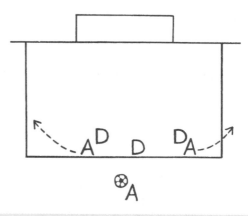

Spreading the defense in front of the goal

Losing a Guard

If a defender is doing her job right, she will make it very difficult for you to even receive the ball, especially when you're right in front of the goal. So you're going to have to figure out a way to lose her. Movement is your best weapon. If you stand still, she can guard you easily. If you run around, she has to follow. And you know where you're going next.

Tip

When you're down in front of the goal, you have to make sure that your runs wide don't put you offside.

She doesn't. Just make sure your moves are quick and sharp. A long, loopy jog around won't give the defender any difficulty.

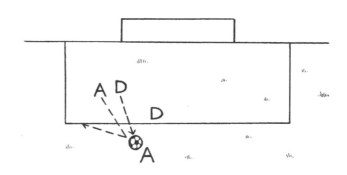

Losing a defender

Look at this figure and you can see one example of how to do this. To start, run straight at the person who is bringing the ball down the field. If your defender follows you, she's leaving space in the goal area.

At some point in your run, stop and run off to the side and back toward the goal. If your teammate is playing heads-up ball, she'll pass right at that moment and you'll have the ball free and clear. Take that shot!

Keep in mind that the success of this play depends as much on the timing of the passer as it does on the running of the receiver. If you're the one with the ball, you have to always be paying attention to your teammates.

Move the Ball

Dribble your way around the cones from START to GOAL. Avoid bumping into other members from your team who are practicing at the same time.

Speed Drill

You're wide open for a pass—what do you do? This tiny picture puzzle shows you!

> Hi! How do you do?

Just for Fun

To spice up the game of soccer a little and give you and your teammates more opportunity to score, throw in a few more soccer balls into a regular game of soccer. Now people really have to be looking up and paying attention to all parts of the field. If you can handle two balls, then add a third. See how many balls you can add to your game without it getting out of control.

Offensive Do's and Don'ts for Restarts

CORNER KICK

DO

- Loft the ball into the center of the goal area
- Use your head to take the the shot
- Move around to get open

DON'T

- Use a kicker who isn't strong enough
- Wait for the ball to land
- Stand in one spot waiting for the ball

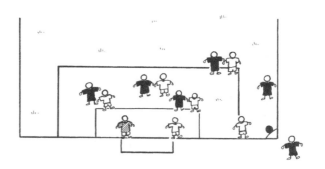

The corner kick

DIRECT KICK

DO

- Take the shot as quickly as possible
- Go for it if you're near the goal

DON'T

- Wait for the defense to set up a wall or mark up (see page 81)
- Waste a shot opportunity by passing it off
- Wait for a whistle—you won't hear one

WORDS to KNOW

restart: Occurs after play has been stopped because of the referee's whistle. Restarts include corner kicks, goal kicks, direct kicks, indirect kicks, kickoffs, and throw-ins.

Offensive Do's and Don'ts for Restarts *(continued)*

INDIRECT KICK

DO

- ⚽ Have one player tap the ball and a second follow behind and shoot it
- ⚽ Take advantage of the other team making a wall by passing to a player on your team who is now open

DON'T

- ⚽ Have your first player shoot it; the goalie can let it in if only one person has touched it, and it won't count as a goal
- ⚽ Treat it like a direct kick and chip it over, well away from the wall

WORDS to KNOW

chip: A sharp, stabbing kick that gives the ball some air and backspin but doesn't give much distance, so the player is able to loft the ball over an opponent's head without the ball going too far.

THROW-INS

DO

- ⚽ Throw it as soon as you can; there's no whistle to wait for unless there is a substitution
- ⚽ Throw it at your teammate's feet
- ⚽ Throw it down the line if you're near your goal
- ⚽ Throw it in the middle if you're near their goal

DON'T

- ⚽ Wait for the defense to set up
- ⚽ Throw it so hard that your teammate can't handle it easily, especially when she's close to you
- ⚽ Throw it down the line if you're in front of the opponent's goal
- ⚽ Throw it in the middle if you're in front of your own goal

The throw-in

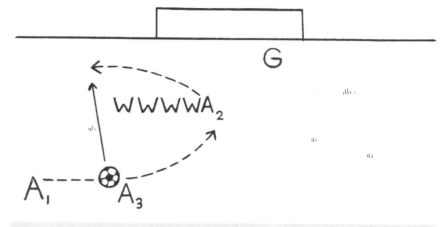

Argentina World Cup play

Opposite Offense

Here's a funny conversation between two soccer players. All the words that are underlined actually mean the opposite! Above each underlined word or group of words, write a word that means the opposite.

"Hey <u>here</u>, Lucas!"

"<u>Good-bye</u>, Caitlin!"

"How are <u>me</u>?"

"<u>You</u> <u>haven't</u> a <u>good</u> <u>hot</u>."

"How <u>wonderful</u>! I hope you <u>give</u> <u>worse</u> <u>a long time from now</u>."

"<u>You</u>, too. I <u>did</u> <u>wake</u> <u>none</u> <u>day</u> <u>short</u>."

"Oh, that's too <u>good</u>. Well, <u>you</u> <u>haven't</u> to <u>come</u>. <u>Hello</u>!"

"<u>Hello</u>. See <u>me</u> <u>sooner</u>."

Open Your Big Mouth

When all is said and done, however, the best offensive weapon you have is your mouth. Talk to your teammates all the time. Let them know if they have time to get the ball under control or if they have to get rid of it quickly. Let them know where you are or where you're going.

Here are some words that are typical soccer terms, and here's what they mean:

1-2: It means the same as *wall.*
Back: "I'm behind you."
Cross it: "Send a lofted ball to the center."
Give-and-go: It means the same as *wall.*
Line (Wing): "I'm on the touchline or sideline."
Man on: "You don't have time to settle the ball.
   There's a player on you."
Square: "I'm at a right angle to you."
Switch the field: "Send the ball to the other side of the field."
Time: "You have time to settle the ball."
Through: "Send a ball in between the two defenders
   and I'll run onto it."
Wall: "Pass it to me, run around the defender, and I'll pass
   it back."

Using these terms helps give your teammate a specific idea of where you are. Just yelling, "I'm open" doesn't help as much. And on the flip side, you should be talking only when you are open. Don't say "square" just to let your teammate know where you are when you have a few defenders between you and the ball.

Just for Fun

To get people in the habit of talking, play a passing game with names. Mark off a fairly large area and divide the group in half. One half should have balls; the other shouldn't. The group with the balls dribbles around the area until they hear someone call their name. Then they pass to that person and run off and find someone with a ball who they can call to. You can take it up a notch by also having people say "square" or "back" for instance, to describe their location, in addition to the name.

Tip

Make sure you're all speaking the same lingo. Don't be yelling "wall" when everyone else on your team calls it "give-and-go."

Chapter 7

Defense

 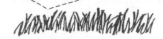
Online Kick

The Soccer Hall of Fame has a great Web site. Go to www.soccerhall.org. In addition to keeping track of all the games for the WUSA, MLS, and the national teams, they have great games to play and they will tell you what happened on this day in soccer history.

Speed Drill

This tiny number puzzle shows a popular kind of defense. What is it?

1 one

Defending the goal is more than just the goalkeeper's job. It's the job of every single player on the field. In fact, if the ball even gets to the goalie, it means that ten other people failed at what they were supposed to be doing.

You have two purposes when you're defending. You want to stop the other team's attack, and you want to take the ball away from them. Working as a team can help you to achieve both of those goals. But first you need to learn the individual defensive skills.

The One-on-One Defender

Good defense starts with good individual skills. Defenders need balance, focus, and patience. Speed, strength, and skills help, too, of course, but that goes for everyone on the field.

Balance is primary. It's tough to stay on a player when he's trying every move in the book, changing speeds, changing directions, and faking you out. You have to react. You have no idea where he's going next. The best way to do this is to stay low, with your legs apart and your knees bent. Your arms should be out rather than at your side. All of this will help you keep your balance as you're forced to change directions quickly.

The defensive stance

Part of defense is focus. You need to have all your attention on the ball. You can't let your mind wander, because you might have to react in a split second. Watch the ball and only the ball. Don't become distracted by the fakes the attacker is trying

to make with her body. It doesn't matter if she's leaning to the left or lunging to the right. If her feet aren't doing anything, then neither is the ball.

And finally, defense is a waiting game. You don't want to make a move until you're sure you can get the ball. If you over commit too early, the dribbler will be around you in a heartbeat. You want to wait for her to make a mistake. The second she lets the ball get a little too far away, pounce on it.

Containment

Sometimes you're not right on top of the ball; instead, you have an attacker coming at you and heading for the goal. In this case, your behavior is slightly different. The first thing you want to do is slow him down. This is especially important if he's on a break-away and you have to wait for the rest of your teammates to catch up and get back to defend. By slowing the attacker down, you're giving your teammates a chance to get back and help.

As the player approaches you, jog in and approach him, too. Notice I said *jog*. You don't want an all-out sprint here because then you'll have a harder time adjusting to what the dribbler does. Your momentum will still be taking you forward. So move in as fast as you can while still being able to stop on a dime.

When you get within 4 or 5 feet of the player, go into your defensive stance. Just like before, stay low, with your knees bent and your legs apart. Keep your arms out wide for balance and to block as much of the attacker's vision as you can. Now back up slowly. The attacker will have to slow down because you're in front of him. This is called **containment**. You have to key on keeping your body between him and the goal. Containment allows your teammates to recover and it also can force the attacker to make a mistake. He might pass the ball too soon or make a dribbling error. Whatever you do, don't move in to steal

Just for Fun

If you and a friend want to practice soccer, a little one-on-one game will help work on lots of skills, especially defense. A piece of advice, though: don't make your goals more than 20 feet apart. You're going to be exhausted. If you have four people, you might want to have two people be the goals (if they spread their legs wide, you can kick it through their legs) and two people play one-on-one. After a goal, you switch up. That way you get some rest because one-on-one is very tiring.

WORDS to KNOW

containment: The process of slowing down an attacker and keeping him in front of you as you back toward the goal.

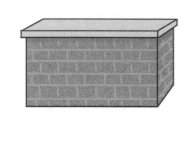
the ball until you're sure you can get it. The last thing you want is to have him fake around you and leave you in the dust.

As you're containing the attacking player, try to push him (not with your arms, but by forcing him with your defending) toward the side. The closer he is to the touchline, the worse his angle is for the goal. Plus, you may be able to trap him against the line or in the corner and force him to kick the ball out-of-bounds. To force him over to the side, you want to angle your body so that the open space is over there.

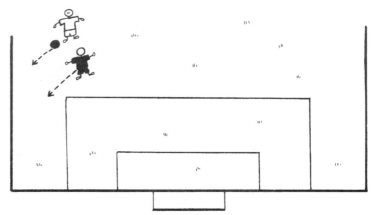

Forcing an attacker to the side

Positions

As I said in the last chapter, everyone plays offense when your team has the ball, and everyone plays defense when you don't. But some positions are generally considered more defensive than others, which is why they are called defenders.

A common field formation is to have four defenders in a diamondlike shape.

The one closest to the midfielders is called the stopper. If your team is **marking up**, which means picking up one of the attacking players and staying with her no matter where she

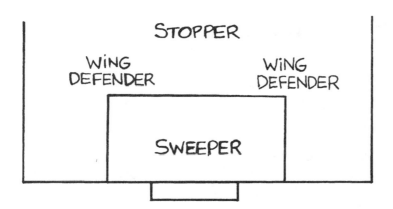

Defensive positions

goes, then the stopper goes with the striker, or center forward. The two defenders out near the touchlines match up with the wing forwards. The sweeper is behind them and doesn't mark anyone. She is there, sweeping back and forth across the field, to pick up anyone who gets free of her defender or any loose balls that might need attention. She's the last-ditch effort before the keeper.

If your team is playing a **zone defense**, then the four defenders cover their area of the field and anyone who comes into it, no matter who it is. The sweeper's job doesn't change, since she was already covering a zone instead of a player.

If you're playing zone, then you need to make sure you communicate well. One person needs to move forward and confront the player with the ball. Usually it's the person defending that zone. She should yell "Ball!" and make her move. Then the rest of the defenders know that they are responsible for covering her area, and they shift accordingly. If the ball is passed into another zone, then somebody else picks up the dribbler and the first defender slips back into zone mode. It takes a lot of teamwork, but it can be a very effective defense.

WORDS to KNOW

marking up: Another term for man-to-man defense. That means you cover a player rather than an area, staying with them no matter where they go.

zone defense: Covering an area rather than a person. You pick up the player who goes into that area.

Tip

When you're defending against a corner kick, you should try to stand slightly in front of the person you're guarding. That way you can get to the ball first. Be careful, however, that she doesn't slip away because she's behind you. Be looking at her out of the corner of your eye.

Defense Against Restarts

After having read the previous chapter on what the offense should be doing, you might be able to figure out what the defense should be doing for the restarts. Match up the kicks in Column A with the defensive response in Column B.

COLUMN A

Corner kick

Direct kick

Indirect kick

Goal kick

Throw-in

COLUMN B

1. Go wide to the touchline. Do not kick the ball in front of the goal.

2. Mark up and look for the ball to come down the line.

3. Set up a wall in front of the kick.

4. Mark up tightly and be prepared for the second kicker to take the shot.

5. One player should take the near post, the goalkeeper should be on the far post, and a defender should be looking for the short ball. Everyone else marks up.

Answer: You probably figured it out on your own, but corner kick goes with #5, direct kick goes with #3, indirect kick goes with #4, goal kick goes with #1, and throw-in goes with #2.

If you'll notice, most of the restarts have you marking up. You should do this even if you're playing a zone defense. Try to steal the ball immediately, and then if that doesn't work, go back into your zone.

Defensive Lineup

This defensive lineup has five players, arranged from shortest to tallest. Read the clues to figure out who plays which position.

The goalie is taller than the wing.
The fullback is taller than the sweeper.
The sweeper is taller than the stopper.
The wing is taller than the fullback.

Patty Ben Jamal Flo Josh

The Wall

Making a wall in front of a direct kick is a valuable defensive tool, but you don't want to use it until you have it mastered. A weak wall is worse than no wall at all, because you've taken four or five of your defensive players and put them all in one spot. Here are the key points.

1. Listen to your goalkeeper. He will tell you how many players he wants in the wall and he will line you up.
2. Stand as close to the kick as you're allowed, which is 10 yards.
3. The end player should be blocking the goalpost on one side. The goalie will tell you to move right or left if you're not right there.
4. Everyone else should line up shoulder-to-shoulder, and so tight that the ball cannot get through.
5. The minute the ball is kicked, break up and defend as normal.

Just for Fun

To practice working with another defender, you might want to try this exercise for four players. Have two players stand on a line (the defenders) and two across from them about 30 feet away (the attackers). The defenders start with the ball and pass it to the attackers. The attackers then try to get the ball back over the line. Meanwhile, the defenders move forward, working together. One of them should call "ball" and move in close to force the player with the ball to make a move. The other defender stays back with an eye on the open attacker, but he is also looking to pick up the one with the ball if he happens to dribble around the first defender. If the defenders get the ball away, they get a point. If the attackers get it over the line, they get a point. Play up to 10 and then switch roles.

A goalie catching a kicked ball

Go Team!

These fans want everyone to know how much they love the game! Follow the directions below to find out their mighty message.

1. Fill in all the blocks on the left side of signs 1, 2, 3, 6, 7, 9, 11, 12, 15, 21
2. Fill in all the top squares on signs 2, 3, 5, 6, 9, 11, 15, 16, 21
3. Fill in all the bottom squares of signs 1, 2, 3, 9, 11, 12, 16
4. Fill in all the right squares of signs 1, 6, 11, 12
5. Fill in all the squares down the middle of signs 5 and 8

6. Fill in the very middle square of signs 1, 6, 7, 16, 21
7. Fill in the square just below the middle square of sign 1
8. Copy sign 9 onto sign 18 and 19
9. Copy sign 5 onto sign 13
10. Copy sign 7 onto sign 10
11. Copy sign 2 onto sign 4 and 20
12. Copy sign 11 onto sign 17 and 14

Use Your Head

A smart heads-up defender can steal a lot of balls by paying attention to what her attackers are doing. If you notice that someone never passes with her left foot, then cut off her right side and force her to use her left. If you have a lot of speed, you can step away from the player you're guarding, leaving her slightly "open" for a pass and then zip in and intercept the pass when it comes. Force the players wide if they don't have a good cross. If the other team is very good, then stay back so they don't get a breakaway. A smart, focused defender is invaluable to her team.

Why do soccer players have such a hard time eating popcorn?

They don't use their hands!

Eddie Pope

Eddie Pope, a defender for the D.C. United team, didn't start out as a defender. He was so fast that most of his coaches thought he should be a forward. He was good but not great in that position, and it wasn't until one coach saw his potential as a defender that Eddie really began to shine. He has since won the Defender of the Year award and has been voted onto the all-star team four years running.

occer can be rough on your body. Sprained ankles, pulled muscles, and lots of bumps and bruises are just part of the game. But it also can be great for you. It builds endurance, improves your coordination, and gets your heart and lungs some good exercise. Whether it makes you hurt or healthy is largely up to you. Knowing your body's needs and limitations is an important part of playing sports. Read this chapter to find out how to deal with some common soccer fitness and injury problems.

First, let's have some fun. Take this little quiz and see how much you already know. You might know more than you think you do. And I'm also willing to bet that a lot of these answers will take you by surprise.

1. How far does a soccer player run in an average soccer game?
   A. 100 yards
   B. 1 mile
   C. 5 miles
   D. As much as a marathon
2. What's the best way to prevent a muscle pull?
   A. Stretch before and after exercising
   B. Lift weights
   C. Sit in front of the TV
   D. Ice your muscles before you play
3. When you're outside playing soccer, when is the best time to drink water?
   A. Before you get thirsty
   B. The minute you feel you're getting thirsty

C. At least an hour after you get thirsty
D. Never, you should drink milk
4. What is the best drink when you're hot and thirsty?
   A. Milk
   B. A sports drink
   C. Soda
   D. Water
5. What is the MOST serious thing that can happen to your body on a hot day?
   A. Sunburn
   B. Heat exhaustion
   C. Heat stroke
   D. Sweat
6. What should you do if you sprain your ankle?
   A. Put ice on it
   B. Elevate it
   C. Wrap it tightly
   D. All of the above
7. What's the worst thing you could do if someone knocks out one of your teeth?
   A. Wash it with warm soapy water
   B. Put it in a glass of milk
   C. Put it in your mouth
   D. Smile
8. Which one of these is NOT a sign of a concussion?
   A. Different-size pupils
   B. Bleeding
   C. Dizziness
   D. Vomiting

The answers are 1–C, 2–A, 3–A, 4–D, 5–C, 6–D, 7–A, 8–B. If you got any of them wrong or even if you didn't, read on for more details about all of those issues and more soccer-related fitness and injury advice.

Getting in Shape

An official soccer game is ninety minutes long. That's ninety minutes of running! One study showed that the average soccer player ran about 5 miles in a game. (But remember, your games won't be that long and you won't have to run that much. If you continue to play, however, you'll build up that kind of endurance.) If you're the kind of kid who's always playing a ton of sports and running around everywhere, then running 5 miles might not seem like too big a deal. But if you take life a little slower, then soccer is something you'll need to build up to.

If you are out of breath in a game, you can find moments when the ball is away from you to take a breather. But don't make the mistake of walking on the field when you should be running. When you're out there, you should be giving it every-thing you've got. It's better to play hard and then come out and rest than to give only half an effort. You won't have as much fun and you won't help your team much. Tell your coach you need a sub. Take a break. Then the next time you go in the game, see if you can push yourself a little more. Eventually, you'll be in the shape you need to be in to be a good player.

You can help yourself get in shape when you're off the field, too. Instead of sitting on the couch watching TV, get outside and do something active. Walk to school instead of getting a ride. Play soccer in the backyard instead of on the computer.

Tip

Many adult soccer players will do weightlifting as part of their exercise routine, but kids shouldn't start until their body is mostly full-grown.

Just for Fun

For one day, keep track of exactly how much you drink. If you have a soda, that's 12 ounces. If you have a big water bottle, that's probably around 20 ounces. A glass of orange juice at breakfast might be about 8 ounces. Add them up and see how well you're doing at keeping your body supplied with liquids.

Stretching

The other great thing you can do for your body is stretch out those muscles. Most kids don't have tight muscles, and in fact most youth leagues can go an entire season without an injury, but it's never too early to get in the habit of stretching. It keeps your muscles loose and flexible, so they won't be caught tight and surprised when you suddenly twist them in a weird direction. Almost every adult soccer player is familiar with the sharp pain of a torn muscle.

Water Works!

Your body is flooded with water. But when you exercise, you lose a lot of that water. You have to make sure that you put it back or your body won't function as well.

So how do you know how much water to drink and when to drink it? The answer will probably surprise you. You have to drink water all the time. You can have eight to ten glasses of water a day and it wouldn't be close to too much. And don't wait until you're thirsty. By that time, your body is aching for water. It doesn't send the thirsty signal until it's feeling mighty dry. So before a soccer match, drink some water. On every break, drink some water. After the game, drink some water. Your body will thank you, and you'll have a lot more energy for the game.

But what if you just can't bear to keep chugging that tasteless, boring, clear liquid anymore? Are you allowed to have sports drinks or some other kind of drink? Well, here's the deal. Water is the best for you, but if you're not getting enough water, then the other drinks are better than nothing. The sports drinks are probably best because they have a lot of water in them. Many of them also have **electrolytes**, which your body loses

when it sweats. So they put that back in your body, which is nice. Soda is not a good idea because the carbonation might make you uncomfortable when you run. Many sodas have caffeine in them too, which will just drain you of water.

Heat Kills

Water will also keep your body cool. If you're playing on a hot day, you need to make sure your body temperature doesn't get too high. This can be extremely dangerous. When your body gets overheated, you can get heat exhaustion or heat stroke. This is especially true on hot, humid days.

Heat exhaustion is the less serious one. It basically means you haven't been doing your job drinking enough water and your body is **dehydrated**. You'll know you have heat exhaustion if you get one of these symptoms:

* Thirst
* Headache
* Dizziness

The cure for dehydration is to stop what you're doing, sit in the shade or get into air conditioning, and slowly drink lots of liquids. Don't gulp. The sudden cold liquid might be too much for your overheated body.

Heat stroke is much more serious. It's a killer. Every year people die from heat stroke: some are hiking in the Grand Canyon without carrying enough water; some are overdressed, overworked, and overweight at midsummer football practices; and some are running marathons and pushing themselves too far to get to the finish line. I have one thing to say to these people and to anyone reading this book: Pay attention to your body's clues!

FUN FACT

Stinky Fact

Have you noticed how grownups get all stinky and sweaty after they work out a lot? And have you noticed that kids don't? That's because until they're teenagers, kids don't have fully developed sweat glands. It's good news because you don't smell, but mostly it means that you have to keep yourself cool in other ways. Take breaks, sit in the shade, and pour water on your head.

WORDS to KNOW

electrolytes: Ions in your body that help control the flow of water throughout the cells.

dehydration: A serious lack of water in your body that can cause a dangerous health situation.

Your body will tell you if it's not working right. Before you even get to heat stroke, you'll probably experience heat exhaustion and the symptoms I told you about there. But if you ignore those and keep pushing yourself, here's what will happen:

- You will run a fever.
- You will stop sweating.
- You will become disoriented.

That last clue is probably the biggest one, but unfortunately if you're the one who is disoriented, you're not going to be able to help yourself too well. So look out for your friends and they'll look out for you. If you see someone with these symptoms, splash them with water, put ice on her neck, and rush her to the hospital. You have to cool her body down before it starts shutting down.

Enough with the really serious, depressing stuff. Most people will drink plenty of fluids and pay attention to what their body is telling them. It's just important for soccer players to know this, since they do a lot of running out in the hot sun.

Online Kick

If you want answers to other health and injury issues, check out *http://dir.yahoo.com/Health/ Diseases_and_Conditions/Sports_ Injuries.* It covers everything else that might happen to you while you're playing soccer.

Ouch!

Heat isn't the only thing that can put a soccer player on the sideline. Injuries are way more often the cause. Muscles get pulled; **ligaments** get stretched or torn; and bumps and bruises pop up everywhere.

Muscles are made up of lots of fibers. They get stretched and pulled every which way when you play soccer. Most of the time they seem to deal with all this activity pretty well, but sometimes the muscle refuses to move and that's when you get a pulled muscle. A pulled muscle is just a tear in the muscle fiber.

ligaments: The connectors between your bones. Ligaments also support organs and connect cartilage to bones.

Warm Up

These two players know that it's important to warm up before a game. Player "L" is going to run slowly around the field, touching all the light colored dots. Player "D" is going to touch all the dark dots on the field. Follow their paths from number to number with your pencil and you will see a winning soccer move!

sprain: A stretching or tearing of a ligament.

As awful as that sounds, it won't be that bad until you're older. Kids have very flexible muscles. You make little tears in your muscles all the time and probably don't even notice them. That's how muscles grow. So slight muscle pulls shouldn't slow you down one bit.

Tip

Once you've sprained something, it's going to be weak. Let it heal completely and strengthen the muscles around it or you could have trouble with it for the rest of your life.

Sprains

Ligaments will give you a little more of a problem. When you stretch your ligaments, it's called a **sprain**. Sprains happen when a joint, like your ankle or your knee, is forced to bend too far or in the wrong way. It's a pretty common soccer injury.

The cure for sprains is a process called RICE. It stands for *Rest, Ice, Compression,* and *Elevation.* That basically means get off your feet, put ice on the injury, wrap it tightly, and put the injured part up so too much blood doesn't flow to the area.

Sometimes a ligament is torn; that's much more serious than a sprain. It might heal itself or you might need surgery. At the very least, your soccer playing is over for the season. Doctors and other people in sports medicine have noticed that girl soccer players tear their knee ligaments way more often than boys. It's the same sport, so why shouldn't the injuries be the same? One theory is that girls' thigh muscles aren't quite as strong, so the knee doesn't have as much support. So, if you're a girl soccer player, work on building up those leg muscles.

Save a Tooth

Every once in a while, players think they're going head to head for a soccer ball and they end up going head to tooth! Ouch! What do you do when a tooth gets knocked out? Believe it or not, a glass of milk is the solution. Put the tooth in milk and rush to the hospital or dentist. If you can't find milk, then pop the tooth in your mouth to keep it wet with your saliva. Just don't swallow it! Whatever you do, however, don't wash the tooth in water. That's a sure way to kill it.

Heads Up!

Because headers are part of the game, at least once a season someone is going to bang you in the head. Most of the time, you'll just say ouch and keep going, but sometimes it's a little more serious than that.

Every time you're hit in the head hard, you have to worry about having a **concussion**. A concussion is basically a brain bruise. Most of the hits to your head will just end up bruising on the surface. The skull does a really good job protecting your brain. But sometimes the hit is so hard, your brain gets a tiny bit injured. That's a concussion, and you have to look out for it.

Some signs of a concussion include:

- Vomiting
- Dizziness or walking unsteadily
- Different-size pupils or pupils that don't react to light
- Talking that makes no sense
- Losing consciousness

If you have a few of these symptoms, get checked by a doctor. The doctor can make sure that you haven't cracked your skull or have bleeding in your brain. If you don't have these symptoms but are still worried because the hit was so hard, have someone keep an eye on you for about a day, looking for what might develop. Even at night, they should wake you up every couple of hours.

WORDS to KNOW

concussion: An injury to the head, particularly the brain, usually involving a loss of consciousness and dizziness. Symptoms can last up to two weeks after the hit and include difficulty following a conversation, headache, sleeping more. The after-effects are called postconcussion syndrome.

Tip

If you have had a really hard blow to the head, stop playing for the day, even if you don't think you have a concussion. A second hit to the same spot could really do some damage.

Body Building

Answer these questions with words that are also names of body parts

1. Twelve inches
2. They hold up a chair
3. Two units of corn
4. Hiding place for treasure
5. A baby cow
6. A tropical tree
7. Part of a comb
8. There are two on a clock
9. Needles have threads in them
10. A unit of lettuce

"I think I'll pass this ball with my 'unit of lettuce'!"

Carla Overbeck

Carla Overbeck is now a defender with the Carolina Courage, but her claim to fame comes as a member of the U.S. National Team. She's played 168 games with that team, including every single World Cup match and every single Olympics. She was a member of the 1991 Women's World Cup Championship team and the 1995 bronze medal team, and captain of the team when they won their second World Cup in 1999.

Game Time Injuries

If you're playing regularly in a soccer league, you're going to see injuries. The younger you are, the fewer you'll see, but you should still know what to do when it happens. If you're injured, sit down. The referee will see you pretty quickly. If someone else is injured, keep playing until the referee blows his whistle. He has to wait until the ball goes out-of-bounds or until the injured person's team has the ball. This is because otherwise someone might cheat (though we certainly hope not!) and fake an injury just as the ball is nearing the goal. Once the whistle is blown, then you can sit down, too, and wait for the coaches and trainers to deal with the injured player. You can even come to the touchline and get a drink if there's enough time. Just don't leave the field, because the clock is still ticking.

Injuries are part of sports, but don't worry. If you're careful, they don't have to be serious. Remember to stretch your muscles, pay attention to what your body is telling you, use RICE when you get an injury, and don't push yourself to play when you've been hurt. There's a great rule of thumb to help you know when to say when. It's called the Five-Minute Rule. If you get hurt or you feel dizzy or anything like that, take a break for five minutes. If you're still not feeling right, then you have a more serious injury and should stop playing. If you feel pretty good, get back in the game!

Chapter 9

Games to Play

The thrill of victory and the agony of defeat. The sweet feeling of success when you score that goal in the last second of play. The dive in the dirt to tip the ball around the goalpost for a save. Let's face it. The drama of competition is half the fun of playing any sport. What are those two competing quotes?

"It doesn't matter if you win or lose, it's how you play the game."

or

"It doesn't matter if you win or lose, as long as you win."

I think most people would agree with a third quote, though:

"It doesn't matter if you win or lose, it's THAT you played the game."

Adding competition makes most sports more fun. Practicing dribbling or trapping or shooting can be fun for a short while, but then it gets dull. You need to have a little challenge.

In each previous chapter there have been small games that you can play with a few people. Here are some games you can play with a lot of players. And don't forget, you can always set up two goals and just have a good old-fashioned soccer game!

Playing for Real

Soccer games are fun, but they teach you real skills. See if you can find fifteen skills hidden in the following letter grid. When you have circled all the skills, read the leftover letters from left to right, top to bottom to find one more!

catch	kick	shoot
defend	pass	stretch
dribble	plan	think
fake	receive	trap
juggle	run	volley

```
C P V O L L E Y T S
R A L O C C E R K D
R E T A I S A I D E
E K C C N P C R A F
L N L E H K I L A E
G I B O I B U T C N
G H O P B V E N N D
U T A L T R E K U O
J S E S H O O T A R
S L H C T E R T S F
```

Cats and Dogs

This is a great game for dribbling and defensive skills, and it can be played with any number of players. You'll need to mark off a playing area, but there are no goals. Divide into two teams: the cats and the dogs. Every player on the cat team should have a ball. The dogs do not have balls.

Someone should have a stopwatch or a watch and say, "Go." At that point, the cats dribble around the playing area, shielding, faking, and turning. In other words, they're doing anything they can to keep the dogs away. The dogs are trying to kick all the balls out of the playing area. When they succeed, stop the watch. Now it's the cats' turn to see if they can beat the time while the dogs do the dribbling.

This is a quick game, so you can trade back and forth four or five times and see who gets the fastest time in the end.

Tip

Instead of calling the teams "Cats" and "Dogs," call them by your favorite MLS or WUSA teams. You can say it's a game of Breakers and CyberRays. Or if you follow World Cup soccer more than U.S. soccer, it can be France against Brazil.

Nothing but Cats

If you don't have a stopwatch, here's a different way to play that game. This time everyone is a cat and out for herself. Each person should have her own ball. Play in the same marked-off area. Now each player not only has to protect and shield her ball, but she also has to try to kick out the other cats' balls. The last player to have her ball in her possession inside the playing area is the winner.

Why do soccer players do well in school?

They know how to use their heads!

Red Rover

Red Rover is another great old game like Red Light, Green Light that can easily be changed to play with a soccer ball. Have a player stand in the middle of a field. He calls, "Red rover, red rover, let white shirts come over!" Then anyone wearing a white shirt has to cross the field dribbling a soccer ball. The object is to get the ball across the field without the person in the middle stealing it. Any player whose ball is stolen goes into the middle to help out on the next "Red Rover" call. You can substitute anything for "white shirts," such as "blond hair" or "blue shorts" or whatever you see on your friends. The last person to get caught is the Red Rover person the next time.

Sink the Subs

Get about eight cones and set them up in an area. These are the subs. One player is the sub commander and tries to keep all the subs "afloat." The other players are the torpedoes, and they try to "sink" the subs by hitting them with their soccer ball. Each time a cone is knocked over, the sub commander tries to put it back up. Play stops if the torpedoes are able to knock down all eight cones (subs) at once. Change sub commanders once all the subs have been sunk and do it again.

SPUD

SPUD is another game that you probably already know, but here's the way you play it with a soccer ball. Give each player a number. Then one player tosses the soccer ball up in the air and calls out a number. Everybody runs away from the ball except the player whose number was called. She runs over and traps the ball out of the air. As soon as she traps the ball, she yells, "Stop!" and everyone else must stop running and freeze where they are.

Now the player with the ball chooses another player to target. She gets two passes to try to hit the player with the ball. Sometimes her first pass may end up nearer another player. It's okay if she changes her target on the second pass. If she hits a

player, then that player gets an *S*. If she doesn't hit anyone, she gets an *S*. If someone already has an *S*, then she gets a *P*, then a *U*, then a *D*, until she has spelled SPUD, at which point she's out of the game.

The person who got the letter throws the ball up and calls out a different number and the game continues.

Run the Gauntlet

Players line up on opposite sides of the field about 30 feet apart; each has a ball. One player stays out of the lineup because he's the one who's going to run the gauntlet. He starts at one end and runs through the two lines of players as they try to pass the ball along the ground and hit him as he runs.

Run the gauntlet

Give each player a turn. If they make it through without being hit, they have to pass the second level. Now they have to run the gauntlet dribbling a soccer ball. I'll bet nobody makes it through that time.

Soccer Golf

To play soccer golf, you first need a "golf" course. That doesn't mean you rush over to the local course and invade it with your soccer balls. You have to be creative. Go to a park. Pick a tree, a fountain, a seesaw, a statue. You'll want at least nine "holes"; eighteen is ideal.

Once your course is set up, it's time to play. Each player should have a soccer ball. It's also handy to have a pencil and a piece of paper to keep score unless you have a really good memory. The first player "tees off" by kicking the soccer ball toward the goal. Then the next player goes. Count how many kicks it takes to hit the "hole." Write that down as your score for that hole. At the end of your course, the player with the lowest score is the winner.

A variation on soccer golf is speedy soccer golf. In this type, it doesn't matter how many kicks it takes for each hole. It just matters how much time you took. So, you use a stopwatch instead of a piece of paper. One person times the other one going through the course, hitting every hole. Then it's the next person's turn to see if she can beat that time.

Soccer-gram

Fill in the answers to the clues, one letter in each numbered space. Then transfer the letters to the boxes above that have the same numbers. When all the boxes are filled correctly, you will have the answer to this riddle:

YUCK!

SQUISH

Why is a soccer field often wet?

A. ___ ___ ___   Easily frighened; timid
     10 2 7

B. ___ ___ ___ ___ ___   Woman on her wedding day
     20 9 19 17 3

C. ___ ___ ___   What a spider builds
     13 8 21

D. ___ ___ ___ ___ ___   One thickness of something
     5 11 15 23 18

E. ___ ___   Short nickname for father
     4 14

F. ___ ___ ___ ___ ___   Place in a barn for a horse
     16 1 6 12 22

1	2	3		4	5	6	7	8	9	10		11	12	13	14	15	16		17	18	19	20	21	22	23

!

Crab Soccer

This game is hilarious. It's also completely exhausting. You thought soccer was tiring? Try crab soccer.

Basically, crab soccer is played just like soccer but with two big differences. The first is that the field is much, much smaller. The second is that you have to play the whole game doing the crab walk. If you don't know what a crab walk is, check out the following figure.

Crab soccer

Soccer Baseball

The more people the better for soccer baseball, and you'll need to have at least ten. Divide into two teams. One team is at bat and the other is out in the field. The fielding team should set up like baseball fielders as in the following figure. If you're not too familiar with baseball, you may want to play another game.

Soccer baseball

If you have only five on a side, you should have a player on first, second, and third base, a pitcher, and an outfielder. The pitcher can cover home plate.

There are a few big differences between baseball and soccer baseball, other than the ball, of course.

1. You never use your hands in soccer baseball.
2. The "batter" must run to every base each time he's up.
3. The fielders must pass the ball to every base and the ball must beat the batter home to get an out.

So that's basically it. The pitcher passes the ball to the batter. The batter kicks it and begins running the bases. If the batter reaches home plate before the ball, his team gets a run. If the ball gets there first, his team gets an out. Three outs and the teams switch sides.

Dodge Ball

You've probably played some form of dodge ball in gym class. Here's how you play it with soccer balls. One player with a ball starts as It. The other players run around in a small marked-off area (such as the 18-yard box if you're on a soccer field). The player who is It must try to hit the other players with the ball. When a player is hit, she must then get a ball and join the first player. The last player left who has not been hit is the winner.

Team Dodge Ball

Here's another variation if you have at least eight or ten players. Divide into two teams. One team should form a big circle. It's best if you can draw the circle or put up cones to mark it. The other team is inside the circle.

The team on the outside has one or more soccer balls. The outside team kicks the soccer balls and tries to hit the players in the middle. When a player gets hit, he must leave the circle. Play ends when all the players have been eliminated. Then the teams switch places.

Square Soccer

Here's a game you can play with fewer people. Set up four cones in a small square and divide your friends into two teams. One team takes two touching sides of the square, and the other team takes the other two sides.

The object of the game is not to let the ball go over the line you're defending. You are not allowed into the square, but you may move up and down your line. If everyone is defending too well, then make it a little more difficult by adding more balls.

Notice that many of these games are variations of games you play on the playground or in gym class. There are probably tons more games you could come up with if you used a little imagination. Soccer tennis? Soccer croquet? The possibilities are endless.

Just for Fun

If you really want to get competitive in this game, you can time how long it takes for a team to be eliminated. Then the other team has to beat that time. Or you could set the time beforehand and see how many people are still in the middle after three minutes, for example.

Online

If you want to know about soccer games for the computer rather than the playing field, check out *http://sgh.soccergaming.com* for reviews on the latest computer games.

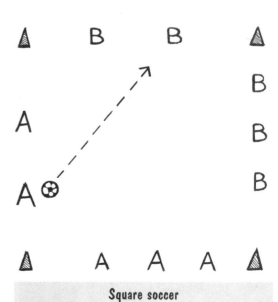

Square soccer

Chapter 10

Going Pro

So you're a master at the game now, right? People can't say enough good things about you. Dynamite dribbler, shooting star, perfect passer, terrific trapper, great goalie, and awesome attacker. It's all true, and you love it. But now what? You've perfected your play, beaten your buddies, and even wrapped up reading this book. You're an expert and ready to hit the big-time.

But then again, maybe you're just a big fan.

Either way, there are lots of professional soccer players and teams that you might want to take a look at. In the United States there are two fairly new professional leagues: the Women's United Soccer Association (WUSA), which is obviously for women, and Major League Soccer (MLS) for men. There are also the men's and women's national teams that take the cream of the crop and send them around the world to represent the United States in international competitions.

All of these teams are really fun to watch, and their history is pretty interesting, too.

Women's United Soccer Association

Women's soccer in the United States has a pretty short history, but what they lack in years, they've certainly made up in ability. Until 1972, when **Title IX** was made into law, there weren't many sports options for girls. There were a few sports (such as field hockey), but soccer usually wasn't one of them.

But in the seventies, things started to change. Towns were realizing that soccer was cheap in terms of equipment and an easy sport for kids to learn. Youth leagues started popping up everywhere. Because of Title IX, there were opportunities for both girls and boys to play. And the girls were off and running.

Title IX: A law passed in 1972 that essentially said that schools couldn't have a sport for boys and not have one for girls if there was an interest.

A Woman's Game

The first record of a women's game was one played in Scotland in the 1600s. This was a game between married women and unmarried women. The married women won.

It turns out that girls all over the world were starting to realize the same thing. This sport is fun! Women's teams started to develop and the level of skill skyrocketed. In 1991, FIFA created the first Women's World Cup. Guess who won? Yup, the United States.

World Cup competition happens every four years, so the next one was in 1995. Unfortunately, the women couldn't repeat (Norway won), but they did pull out a respectable third-place bronze medal win. A year later in 1996, women's soccer was an Olympic event and again the U.S. women proved that they were tops, coming home with the gold. The country was beginning to notice them. When the 1999 World Cup began, it became obvious that the women's soccer team had developed quite a following. They had 90,000 fans in the stadium watching their nail-biting final match against China and another 40 million watching them on TV. Their victory made them the nation's darlings.

Not wanting to lose this momentum, some of the top players and a number of investors decided that they would form a professional women's league: The Women's United Soccer Association (WUSA). They decided to start small—eight teams in eight cities:

Winning Women

"The future of football is feminine."
—Joseph S. Blatter, the current president of FIFA, after the 1999 Women's World Cup

Atlanta Beat

Bay Area CyberRays

Boston Breakers

Carolina Courage

New York Power

Philadelphia Charge

San Diego Spirit

Washington Freedom

It took about a year to put it all together, but on April 14, 2001, the first game of the WUSA was played. It was between the Bay Area CyberRays and the Washington Freedom, with the Washington Freedom coming out on top.

 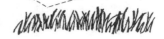

Online Kick

To learn more about WUSA, you can visit their Web site at *www.wusa.com*. You can chat with some of your favorite players, see the schedules for upcoming games, and answer opinion polls. And that's just the beginning.

Where do soccer players dance?

At a football!

WORDS to KNOW

World Cup: The ultimate soccer trophy. The team that wins the World Cup competition is considered the best soccer team in the world.

Do you have a team near you? If the league is a success, what other cities around the country would be good places for the women's league to expand? List five cities and come up with good names to go with them. Maybe the WUSA will take your suggestions!

_____

_____

_____

_____

_____

If you don't have a WUSA team near you, you can watch some of their games on television. Watching the pros play will definitely help you improve your game. Then maybe someday you can be the one on TV.

Major League Soccer

Major League Soccer (MLS) has been around a little longer than the WUSA, but it's still, like the United States, a newcomer to the soccer scene. The United States wanted to host the 1994 **World Cup** but having its own professional soccer league was part of the deal.

At one time, the United States had a professional league, the NASL or North American Soccer League, but it turned out to be a disaster. The NASL disbanded in 1984 after losing tons of money. Unless something radically different occurred, a new league would have a hard time getting investors. But Alan I.

Rothenberg, the chairman of U.S. Soccer, decided that it could be done, and in 1993 the MLS was born. Even so, a lot of planning had to happen before the league became a reality on the playing field. In fact, the first game wasn't played until 1996.

The first part of the MLS grand plan was to keep the number of teams pretty small. That way, the teams would all have top-quality players and be able to put on a good show for the fans. After all, isn't that what professional sports teams are there for? The failed NASL was in twenty-six cities and the teams were just not very good.

The MLS decided to start with ten teams, and now they're up to twelve: Here are the current twelve teams:

Chicago Fire	Los Angeles Galaxy
Colorado Rapids	Miami Fusion
Columbus Crew	New England Revolution
Dallas Burn	New York/New Jersey MetroStars
D.C. United	San Jose Earthquakes
Kansas City Wizards	Tampa Bay Mutiny

The Chicago Fire and the Miami Fusion are the new teams, added in 1998.

Next the MLS had to find the players. This was supposed to be a U.S. league, so you'd think there would be U.S. citizens playing in it. But here was the difficulty. Most of the other countries in the world have better players than the United States, so if good money was being offered, those foreign players would probably want to try out for the MLS teams and beat out a lot of the U.S. players. That's what happened in the NASL. Almost all the players were from other countries, which may have been the reason there wasn't a lot of fan support. The fans simply didn't know who the players were.

Jokin' Around

Some flies were playing football in a saucer, using a sugar lump as a ball.

One of them said, "We'll have to do better than this, lads. We're playing in the cup tomorrow."

Online Kick

Go to *www.mlsnet.com* for all the news in Major League Soccer. They have reports on each game, profiles of your favorite players, and much, much more.

 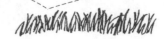

FUN FACT

The First MLS Player

On January 3, 1995, Tab Ramos, a star on the national team, was the first player to be signed for the brand-new Major League Soccer. He was assigned to the New York/New Jersey MetroStars and still plays for them.

Just for Fun

Have your coach look into the MLS high-five club. If you have an MLS team near you, your youth team might be able to go down on the field before the game. The youth teams line up on the grass before the game and high-five the MLS players as they take the field. Then you go back to your seats and root for the team to win.

But the league didn't want to ban foreign players completely. These players were highly skilled and would bring up the level of play considerably. So the league decided that only five international players could be on the roster for each team. The rest would have to be from the United States.

Finally, on April 6, 1996, the MLS played its first game. The San Jose Clash went up against D.C. United. It was as exciting as the founders had hoped, a nail biter to the end. The score was 0–0 up until the last two minutes when the Clash's Eric Wynalda scored, giving the Clash the league's first victory. The Clash are now known as the San Jose Earthquakes.

The MLS season ends with the MLS Cup. That first year it went to D.C. United.

So far MLS has been a limited success. It's not bringing in tons of money, but the fan base is increasing every year. League promoters are hoping that young players like you will make soccer as popular in this country as it is in the rest of the world.

The National Teams

The ultimate soccer team for either a man or a woman is the national team. Even players who are on an MLS team or a WUSA team try out for the national teams. These teams are made up of the top twenty players in a country, and they represent the country in international competitions. Players have to be citizens of the country they play for, but they don't have to have been born there.

The national teams represent the United States in World Cup and Olympic competitions. These competitions are held just once every four years, although they are on different four-year schedules. See if you know enough about soccer to match up the events with the last three times they've been played:

A. World Cup	1. 1992, 1996, 2000
B. Summer Olympics	2. 1991, 1995, 1999
C. Women's World Cup	3. 1990, 1994, 1998

The answer is A–3, B–1, C–2.

Countries take turns hosting these three international events. But it is a huge undertaking to host such a competition. Many games are played, and obviously every game needs a stadium. A lot of countries aren't capable of handling the crowds, but they still want to host the competition. As a result, for the first time in World Cup history, the 2002 World Cup will be held in two countries: Korea and Japan. Each country will have ten cities hosting games.

As you can see, the World Cup is a pretty big undertaking. And believe it or not, many countries have already been weeded out. There are close to two hundred countries that have national teams, but only thirty-two get to the World Cup. So who are the lucky ones?

Online Kick

To read more about the Korea/Japan 2002 World Cup, go to *www.fifaworldcup.com*.

FUN FACT

Talk About New!

On the 1998 U.S. National Team, one player became a U.S. citizen only a week before the World Cup began!

World Cup Veterans

Two players have played in five World Cup tournaments. One is Antonio Carbajal of Mexico who played in 1950, 1954, 1958, 1962, and 1966, and the other is Lothar Matthäus of Germany who played in 1982, 1986, 1990, 1994, and 1998. Lothar played the most World Cup matches—twenty-five.

Brandi Chastain

In 1999, Brandi Chastain was one of the most recognized soccer players in the United States. She had scored the fifth and final goal in the shootout of the World Cup finals against China giving the U.S. team the victory. Thrilled, she ripped her shirt off over her head in the traditional soccer celebration and her picture was captured for the cover of newspapers and magazines all over the country. Brandi currently plays defense and midfield for the Bay Area CyberRays.

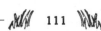

WORDS to KNOW

qualifying matches: Soccer games between countries to determine the top thirty soccer teams in the world for the World Cup.

FuN FACT

World Cup Groupings

The qualifying teams find out their group about six months before the World Cup. Then they're not allowed to play the other three teams in their group until the World Cup. They usually try to set up matches with teams that have similar styles, though.

Well, first of all, the country that hosts the World Cup automatically gets in. That's one team (or two in 2002). Then the defending champions automatically get in. The rest of the teams have to earn their spot by playing **qualifying matches**.

FIFA divides the world into ten divisions. Then each team in that division plays qualifying matches against the other teams in that division. When the matches are all done, the top three teams in each division qualify for the World Cup—in addition to the other two teams (the defending champs and the host).

Then the World Cup begins. The teams are divided into eight groups with four teams each. FIFA looks at the scores and the win/loss records of all the qualifying matches and then spreads the top teams throughout the eight groups, so they aren't all playing each other in the first round.

Finally it's June, and it's time for the World Cup competition to begin. The first round of the tournament is played as a round robin. Each team plays the other three teams in the group. The two teams that come out of that little competition with the best record move on. So, to do the math for you, sixteen teams move on and sixteen are eliminated.

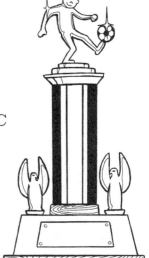

Now it's single-elimination time. The winner of group A plays the runner-up of group B. The winner of group B plays the runner-up of group A. The winner of group C plays the runner-up of group D, and so on. The teams play one game, and the winners of that game move on. Now we're down to eight teams, and it's single elimination the rest of the way until there's one final winner.

Here are the winning countries since the World Cup began in 1930:

1930: Uruguay
1934: Italy
1938: Italy
1942: No World Cup because of World War II
1946: No World Cup because of World War II
1950: Uruguay
1954: West Germany
1958: Brazil
1962: Brazil
1966: England
1970: Brazil
1974: West Germany
1978: Argentina
1982: Italy
1986: Argentina
1990: Germany
1994: Brazil
1998: France

Here are the winning countries for the Women's World Cup, which began in 1991:

1991: United States
1995: Norway
1999: United States

Landon Donovan

Landon Donovan is the great soccer hope for the U.S. National Team for the World Cup in 2002. Some people say he's the best American soccer player ever. The first time he played for the national team he scored a goal, becoming only the sixth person ever to do that. When he's not playing for the U.S. team, he's a forward for the San Jose Earthquakes and a star in that league. In the 2001 All-Star Game, he scored four goals, something that's never been done before.

Manager: I'll give you fifty dollars a week to start, and a hundred dollars a week in a year's time.

Young player: OK, I'll come back in a year's time!

World Cup Crossword

Figure out the answers to the questions below and fill them into the numbered crossword grid. All the answers will have to do with the great soccer info you learned while enjoying this book!

ACROSS

1. "_____ makes perfect!"
4. You can easily trap the ball here (between the head and the waist).
7. Short pass made using the inside of the foot (2 words).
10. If you get a ____ card, you are out of the game!
11. Keeping your body between the ball and another team's player.
14. Playing soccer is a lot of _____!
15. "I'm at a right angle to you!"
16. If you are attacking the goal, you are on _____.
20. Oops! You are between the opponent and the ball, and you're not going for the ball!
23. The most important soccer drink.
24. Look like you're going left, but you are really going right.
25. The other kids you play soccer with.
27. The ultimate soccer trophy (2 words).
28. The most important piece of soccer equipment.
29. What the ref blows.
30. "I'm behind you!"
31. Another name for the goalie.

DOWN

1. Most famous soccer player from Brazil.
2. To get a flying ball under control, you must _____ it.
3. Ouch! You stretched a ligament and have a bad _____.
5. Another name for an instep pass is a "_____ pass."
6. When a player kicks the ball out of the air.
8. These keep the part of your leg below the knee safe.
9. Jesters do this with three balls, but soccer players do it with only one!
12. The most basic soccer rule: NO _____!
13. If you're protecting the goal, you're on _____.
17. Another name for a "forward."
18. What they call soccer in other countries.
19. A player might run _____ miles in a soccer game!
21. Do this to keep your muscles flexible and soft.
22. If you knock the ball over your own goal line, the other team gets a _____ (2 words).
24. Action that is not allowed.
26. Don't wait! Rush up to _____ the ball.
27. Initials for the women's professional soccer league.

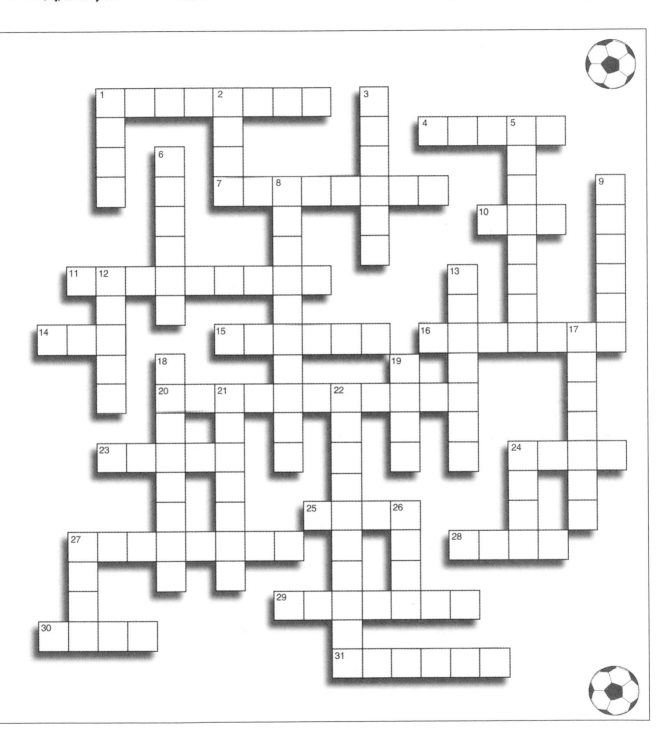

Tryout Tips

Are you worried about upcoming tryouts? Nothing is more intimidating than lining up with a bunch of other kids who are getting ready to show off their soccer skills. Who plays which position? Have they been training? What secrets do they know about the game that you don't? Relax! Every other person there is wrestling with the same uncertainties and nerves.

Tips for a Great Tryout

Relax. You know that you have great skills if you perform to the best of your abilities. Keep that in mind and take a deep breath. Now go out and give it your best effort. Remember, nerves have an uncanny ability to cause mistakes. Coaches will take that into consideration, but do your best to keep those butterflies in your stomach still!

Be positive. No matter what happens during tryouts, maintain a positive attitude and disposition. If you make a mistake, ask the coach for advice. Analyze the play and see what you can do to make sure that the mistake isn't repeated. Everyone makes mistakes. However, players that shake it off and keep working hard show a maturity and sportsmanship that is admired by everyone.

Work with the other players. Soccer is a game that requires teamwork. Don't be so busy showing off your own skill that you forget that there are other players on the field. No one likes a ball hog. Use your ability to work with your teammates. If your teammate has a better shot, pass the ball. This shows smart playing. After all, you're all after the same goal!

Get in shape. If you can show your coach that you've been working hard on your own time, it will reflect well in tryouts. Coaches are looking for kids that are dedicated enough to stay in shape. Plus, it doesn't hurt to be the first one to finish a fitness test!

Bring on the moves. Your coach will be impressed with your new ball handling

tricks. Don't be afraid to show them off. Remember, soccer is a game of both skill and smarts. If you can show the coach that you know the game, recognize the strategy, and can play intelligently, the lasting impression is sure to be a positive one.

Get enough sleep. We all know that an early bedtime is for younger kids, but if you want to succeed in the tryouts, you need to be on top of your game. Get plenty of sleep the night before tryouts to ensure that you're well rested and ready to play a good game of soccer. A good night's sleep will keep you alert, energized, and positive throughout the tryouts.

Be a good listener. Coaches want players that can listen and learn. Listen closely when your coach gives you instruction. He or she may be testing your ability to understand simple instructions.

Be prompt. Coaches like players who arrive on time and ready to play. Don't show up right when tryouts start and begin getting ready. If you need the time to put on your shin guards and shoes, arrive early. Also, this will give you some extra time to warm up and calm your nerves.

Be willing to try new things. If the coach asks you to try a drill you've never done, let alone never heard of, be open and willing to try it. If you don't understand, ask questions. A coach is there to help you learn

and improve. Be willing to try a new move, or a new shot on the goal. You may even find that you like it!

Be health-conscious. Make sure that you eat a nutritious meal a few hours before the tryouts, and bring lots of water. You'll need the water to stay hydrated and alert.

Come prepared. Make a checklist the day before tryouts detailing everything you need to bring. Socks, shoes, shin guards, water, a special shirt, shorts, etc. Check it off right before you leave for the tryouts. Coming prepared makes a good impression on any coach.

Be friendly. Part of what makes a great team is how everyone works together. Be nice to the other players, get to know them, and help out when asked. Coaches appreciate players with a positive attitude who are friendly with each other. If you don't know all of the other players, introduce yourself. Strike up a conversation. You can always ask the person where she's from, what position she plays, or if she's nervous too! You may find that you've got a new friend.

Have fun! You're trying out for the team because you love soccer. Going to tryouts shouldn't be a chore. Rather, it allots you a couple of hours to have some fun playing a game that you enjoy. Coaches like a player that has a love of the game. This indicates a willingness to learn and succeed.

National Soccer Hall of Famers

If you practice really hard, maybe someday your name will end up on this list! These Hall of Fame players are not chosen from skill alone, but also for their integrity, sportsmanship, and character—both on and off the field.

1950
Jock Ferguson
Billy Gonsalves
Sheldon Govier
Millard Lang
Robert Millar
Harry Ratican
Dick Spalding
Archie Stark
Peter Wilson

1951
Harold Brittan
Davey Brown
William Fryer
John McGuire
Robert Morrison
Peter Renzulli
Thomas Swords

1952
George Tintle

1953
Jimmy Douglas
John Jaap

1954
Aldo "Buff" Donelli

1955
Thomas Dugan

1958
Francis Ryan

1959
Ralph Carrafi

1963
Rudy Kuntner

1965
Fred Beardsworth
Teddy Glover

1966
Stan Chesney

1968
Arnie Oliver

1971
Gene Olaf
Bert Patenaude

1973
Josef Gryzik

1974
Nick DiOrio
Jimmy Dunn
Werner Mieth

1976
Walter Bahr
Frank Borghi
Charlie Colombo
Geoff Coombes
Robert Craddock Jr.
Joe Gaetjens
Gino Gard
Harry Keough
Joseph Maca
Edward McIlveney
Gino Pariani
Edward Souza
John Souza
Frank Wallace
Adam Wolanin

1977
Jack Hynes
Ben McLaughlin

1978
Raymond Bernabei
Al Zerhusen

1979
Al Harker

1980
John Boulos

1982
Joseph Carenza

1983
George Barr

1986
Andrew Auld
Mike Bookie
James Brown
Thomas Florie
Jimmy Gallagher
James Gentle
Bart McGhee
George Moorhouse
Philip Slone
Ralph Tracey
Frank Vaughn
Alexander Wood

1989
Walter Dick
Bob Gormley
Werner Roth
Willy Roy

1990
Shamus O'Brien

1991
Rudy Getzinger

1992
Chico Chacurian
Werner Fricker

1993
John Nanoski
Pelé

1994
Pat McBride
Lloyd Monsen

1995
Robert Annis
George Brown
Willy Schaller

1996
Nick Kropfelder
Len Oliver

1997
Paul Danilo
Alex Ely
Johnny Moore
Jimmy Roe

1998
F. Beckenbauer
April Heinrichs
Ed Murphy

2000
Giorgio Chinaglia
Carin J. Gabarra

2001
Rick Davis
Bill Looby

Glossary

chip: A sharp, stabbing kick that gives the ball some backspin but doesn't give much distance, so the player is able to loft the ball over an opponent's head without the ball going too far.

concussion: An injury to the head, particularly the brain, usually involving loss of consciousness and dizziness.

containment: The process of slowing down an attacker and keeping him in front of you as you back toward the goal.

cross: A high lofted pass into the center of the field in front of the goal. The ideal cross should come down in the vicinity of a teammate's head. Then she can put her forehead on it and redirect it into the goal.

dehydration: A serious lack of water in your body that can cause a dangerous health situation.

dribbling: A series of short, crisp taps on the ball that allows the soccer player to run with the ball under his control.

electrolytes: Ions in your body that control the flow of water throughout the cells.

FIFA: The Fédération Internationale de Football Association is the official soccer organization for world play. If a rule change is made, it's made by FIFA.

follow through: A term used in many sports. It means that the swinging motion doesn't stop with impact. The leg (or baseball bat or tennis racket) continues to move forward in the same direction.

goal line: Also known as the end line. One of the two shorter lines that form the boundaries of the field of play. The lines are included as part of the field.

half-volley: A shot in which the player kicks the ball after it has bounced. The ball is still in the air but only a bit off the ground.

handling the ball: Or handball. A player can't touch the ball with any part of his arm between the shoulder and fingertips. If he does and the referee thinks he meant to do it, she will call a foul and award a direct kick to the other team.

instep: The arched middle portion of the foot directly in front of the ankle and under the shoelaces.

instep pass: Or shoelace pass. A powerful pass that lets the player loft the ball into the air by striking it with her instep.

juggling: Keeping the ball from touching the ground using your feet and thighs and even your head to pop the ball back up into the air.

ligaments: The connectors between your bones. Ligaments also support organs and connect cartilage to bones.

marking up: Another term for man-to-man defense. That means you cover a player rather than an area, staying with him no matter where he goes.

MLS: Major Soccer League. The MLS is the professional men's soccer league in the United States.

obstruction: This call means you've placed your body between your opponent and the ball without going after the ball yourself. You might be trying to keep your opponent from saving the ball if it's going out-of-bounds or to give your goalie a chance to pick it up. Either way, it's not allowed. You can throw your body in front of another player, however, as long as you're actually going after the ball.

plant: A step toward the ball that shifts your weight forward and gives you more power for your kick.

push pass: A short accurate pass using the inside of the foot.

qualifying matches: Soccer games between countries to determine the top thirty soccer teams in the world.

restart: Occurs after play has been stopped because of the referee's whistle. Restarts include corner kicks, goal kicks, direct kicks, indirect kicks, kick-offs, and throw-ins.

shielding: The process of keeping your body between the defender and the ball to prevent the defender from getting to the ball.

sprain: A stretching or tearing of a ligament.

striker: Another term for the center forward.

Title IX: A law passed in 1972 that essentially said that schools couldn't have a sport for boys and not have one for girls if there was an interest.

touchline: Also known as the sideline. One of the two longer lines that are the boundaries of the field of play. The lines are included as part of the field of play.

trapping: Stopping the soccer ball and getting it under control with any part of the body.

volley: A shot in which the player kicks the ball out of the air.

wall pass: Also called the give-and-go or the 1–2 pass, it is a way of getting around a defender by "bouncing" the ball off one of your teammates. Your teammate receives the ball while you run around the defender and then passes it back to you when you're free.

wing: Sometimes coaches will refer to a forward as a wing or a striker. The wings play out near the touchline, while the striker is another term for the center forward.

World Cup: The ultimate soccer trophy. The team that wins the World Cup competition is considered the best soccer team in the world.

WUSA: The Women's United Soccer Association. The WUSA is the professional women's soccer league in the United States.

zone defense: Covering an area rather than a person. You pick up the player who goes into that area.

PUZZLE ANSWERS

page 5 • **Spelling Ball**

ALIVE	PAL(S)	SILVER
EVIL	PALE	SLAP
LAP	PALER	SLIVER
LEAR	PERT	TOIL
LION	PET	TOIL
LIVE	REAL	TON
LIVER	REAP	VELVET
NOISE	REAPER	VETO
NOT	RELIVE	VISION
NOTE	REVOTE	VOTE
OVER	SEAL	VOTER

10-letter bonus word: television

page 7 • **Let's Play**

1. CLOCK
2. FIELD
3. REFEREE
4. BALL
5. TEAM
6. WHISTLE

BONUS: CLEATS

page 25 • **Speed Drill**
Answer: wide open

page 24 • **Skill Master**

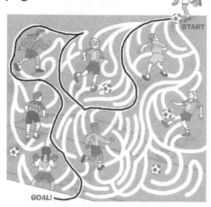

page 30 • **I Spy Soccer**

```
S R O S O S O C C E
O O R O S O C C E S
C E C C O C C O R O
C S O C E C E S O C
R O S E R E R O S S
S S O C C O S E O O
O C C S O C E C C C
C E R O C O C C C E
C O O C S E O O S E
E C O S R O C C O S
```

page 35 • **Fast Pass**

page 27 • **Skill Master Questions**

1. 7
2. 4
3. spiral
4. top left corner
Bonus: 8 and 3

page 33 • **Speed Drill**
Answer: a plant

PUZZLE ANSWERS

page 41 • Teamwork

A	B	
YEE	BID	EYELID
ORF	ROT	FORBID
NPA	AGE	PANTRY
ONT	FIT	NOTICE
RAC	TRY	CARROT
OTC	LID	COTTON
AMN	ICE	MANAGE
UTO	TON	OUTFIT

page 55 • Uniform Uniforms

A B C B
C A Today's Goalie

page 47 • Practice, Practice, Practice

B	F			T		O		T	I			O	C		E		P	U		3	
I	E		S	N	D	O	A	F	G	H	T	E		S	O	U	C	R		Y	O	O	A	E	I	Y	
D	H	E	Y	O	U	T	D	O	O	O	H	E	D		F	G	N	A	A	N	T	E	L	Y	B	L	L
T	A	Y	A	E	S	W	R	F	I	T	T	H	S	I	M	O	R	T	H	R	W	H	L	E	W	E	R	O

IF YOU DO THIS FOR A WHOLE 30
DAYS STRAIGHT, I GUARANTEE BY
THE END OF THE MONTH YOU WILL
BE A TWO-FOOTED SOCCER PLAYER.

page 52 • Keep Your Eye on the Ball

D
FOOT TE
W B DD T
PINGPONG E
F O W H
F L L E
L F I R
TEE SNOW
E N
N B
N BASKET
I S
SOCCER

page 60 • Speed Drill
Answer: in the box

page 62 • We're with You

23 1 25 20 15 7 15 7 15 1 12 9 5

W A Y T O G O, G O A L I E !

PUZZLE ANSWERS

page 71 • **Move the Ball**

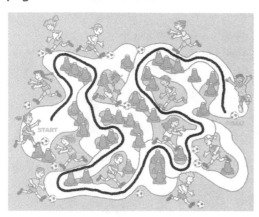

page 71 • **Speed Drill**

Answer: meet the ball

page 74 • **Opposite Offense**

"Hey ~~here~~ *there*, Lucas!"

"~~Good-bye~~ *Hello*, Caitlin!"

"How are ~~me~~ *you*?"

"~~You haven't~~ *I have* a ~~good~~ *bad* ~~hot~~ *cold*."

"How ~~wonderful~~ *awful*! I

hope you ~~give~~ *get* ~~worse~~ *better*

~~a long time from now~~ *soon*."

"~~You~~ *Me*, too. I ~~did~~ *didn't* ~~wake~~ *sleep*

~~none~~ *all* ~~day~~ *night* ~~short~~ *long*."

"Oh, that's too ~~good~~ *bad*.

Well, ~~you haven't~~ *I have* to

~~come~~ *go*. ~~Hello~~ *goodye*!"

"~~Hello~~ *Good-bye*. See ~~me~~ *you* ~~sooner~~ *later*."

page 78 • **Speed Drill**

Answer: one on one

page 80 • **Speed Drill**

Answer: the wall

page 82 • **Defensive Lineup**

The goalie, Josh, is the tallest.
The wing is Flo.
The fullback is Jamal.
The sweeper is Ben.
The stopper, Patty, is the shortest.

page 84 • **Go Team!**

WE GET A
KICK OUT
OF SOCCER

page 93 • **Warm Up**

PUZZLE ANSWERS

page 96 • Body Building

1. Twelve inches	foot
2. They hold up a chair	legs
3. Two units of corn	ears
4. Hiding place for treasure	chest
5. A baby cow	calf
6. A tropical tree	palm
7. Part of a comb	tooth
8. There are two on a clock	hands
9. Needles have threads in them	eyes
10. A unit of lettuce	head

page 98 • Playing for Real

Extra letters spell:
Soccer is all about control!

page 102 • Soccer-gram

A. $\underset{10}{S}\ \underset{2}{H}\ \underset{7}{Y}$ Easily frighened; timid

B. $\underset{20}{B}\ \underset{9}{R}\ \underset{19}{I}\ \underset{17}{D}\ \underset{3}{E}$ Woman on her wedding day

C. $\underset{13}{W}\ \underset{8}{E}\ \underset{21}{B}$ What a spider builds

D. $\underset{5}{L}\ \underset{11}{A}\ \underset{15}{Y}\ \underset{23}{E}\ \underset{18}{R}$ One thickness of something

E. $\underset{4}{P}\ \underset{14}{A}$ Short nickname for father

F. $\underset{16}{S}\ \underset{1}{T}\ \underset{6}{A}\ \underset{12}{L}\ \underset{22}{L}$ Place in a barn for a horse

THE PLAYERS ALWAYS DRIBBLE!

page 114 • World Cup Crossword

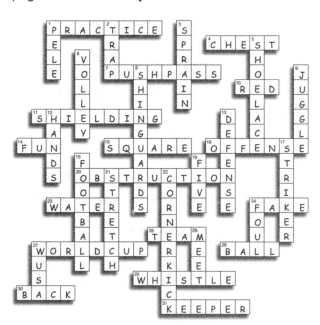

Index

THE EVERYTHING® KIDS' SERIES!

Packed with tons of information, activities, and puzzles, the Everything® Kids' books are perennial bestsellers that keep kids active and engaged. Each book is 8" x 9 ¼", 144 pages, and two-color throughout.

All this at the incredible price of $6.95!

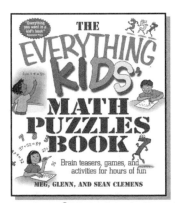

The Everything® Kids' Math Puzzles Book
1-58062-773-0

The Everything® Kids' Bugs Book
1-58062-892-3

The Everything® Kids' Baseball Book, 2nd Ed.
1-58062-688-2

The Everything® Kids' Cookbook
1-58062-658-0

The Everything® Kids' Joke Book
1-58062-686-6

The Everything® Kids' Monsters Book
1-58062-657-2

The Everything® Kids' Mazes Book
1-58062-558-4

The Everything® Kids' Money Book
1-58062-685-8

The Everything® Kids' Nature Book
1-58062-684-X

The Everything® Kids' Puzzle Book
1-58062-687-4

The Everything® Kids' Science Experiments Book
1-58062-557-6

The Everything® Kids' Soccer Book
1-58062-642-4

The Everything® Kids' Travel Activity Book
1-58062-641-6

The Everything® Bedtime Story Book

by Mark Binder

The Everything® Bedtime Story Book is a wonderfully original collection of 100 stories that will delight the entire family. Accompanied by charming illustrations, the stories included are retold in an exceptionally amusing style and are perfect for reading aloud. From familiar nursery rhymes to condensed American classics, this collection promises to promote sweet dreams, active imaginations, and quality family time.

Trade Paperback, $12.95
1-58062-147-3, 304 pages

The Everything® Mother Goose Book

by June Rifkin

The Everything® Mother Goose Book is a delightful collection of 300 nursery rhymes that will entertain adults and children alike. These wonderful rhymes are easy for even young readers to enjoy-and great for reading aloud. Each page is decorated with captivating drawings of beloved characters. Ideal for any age, *The Everything® Mother Goose Book* will inspire young readers and take parents on an enchanting trip down memory lane.

Trade Paperback, $12.95
1-58062-490-1, 304 pages

The Everything® Fairy Tales Book

by Amy Peters

Take your children to magical lands where animals talk, mythical creatures wander freely, and good and evil come in every imaginable form. You'll find all this and more in *The Everything® Fairy Tales Book*, an extensive collection of 100 classic fairy tales. This enchanting compilation features charming, original illustrations that guarantee creative imaginations and quality family time.

Trade Paperback, $12.95
1-58062-546-0, 304 pages

Available wherever books are sold!
To order, call 800-872-5627, or visit us at everything.com

Everything® is a registered trademark of Adams Media Corporation.